CONCILIUM

concilium 1997/3

THE CHURCH IN FRAGMENTS: TOWARDS WHAT KIND OF UNITY?

Edited by

Giuseppe Ruggieri and
Miklós Tomka

SCM Press · London
Orbis Books · Maryknoll

Published by SCM Press Ltd, 9–17 St Albans Place, London N1
and by Orbis Books, Maryknoll, NY 10545

Copyright © Stichting Concilium

English translations © 1997 SCM Press Ltd and Orbis Books, Maryknoll

ISBN: 0 334 03044 7 (UK)
ISBN: 1 57075 128 5 (USA)

Typeset at The Spartan Press Ltd, Lymington, Hants
Printed by Biddles Ltd, Guildford and King's Lynn

Concilium Published February, April, June, October, December.

Contents

Editorial
GIUSEPPE RUGGIERI AND MIKLÓS TOMKA   vii

I · The Situation   1

The Fragmentation of Experience in the Modern World   3
MIKLÓS TOMKA

The God of Christians and the Fragmentation of the
Postmodern World   16
JOHANN REIKERSTORFER

Current Theological Discussion on the Unity of the Church   23
ANGELO MAFFEIS

II · The Past   33

Is the New Testament Canon the Basis for a Church in
Fragments?   35
HANS DIETER BETZ

A Lost Fragment: Jewish Christianity   47
ULRICH H. J. KÖRTNER

In the Footsteps of the Apostolic Churches: Fragmentation
and Unity in the Christian West   55
LORENZO PERRONE

Heresies in the Middle Ages: 'There are Two Churches'   65
ANNE BRENON

Why Did Jansenism Want 'Catholicity' for Itself?   71
BERNARD PLONGERON

III · The Planetary Horizon   79

The Fragment and the Part: An Indic Reflection   81
RAIMON PANIKKAR

Latin America: Against the Threat to the Whole of Life   88
    PAULO SUESS
The Unity of the Church: Women's Experience   95
    LISA SOWLE CAHILL

IV · Perspectives   101
Does the Nature of the Church Call for Unified and Clear
Dogmas?   103
    PIERRE VALLIN
The Unity of the Believer in Question   111
    JEAN-PIERRE JOSSUA
The Pilgrim State of the Christian Church   116
    GREGORY BAUM
Fragments and Forms: Universality and Particularity Today   122
    DAVID TRACY
Towards What Unity of the Churches?   130
    JOHANNES BROSSEDER
The Passion for Unity   139
    JOSEPH MOINGT
The Unity of the Church through the Unity of Humankind   146
    GIUSEPPE RUGGIERI

Contributors   155

Editorial

The subject of this issue combines a statement with a question.

The statement is about the current situation of the churches and the Christians within them. It is easier to make this statement in negative than in positive terms: the churches do not give the impression of being coherent entities. Their most evident aspect is the persistence of division between Christians at the end of a century which has been so rich in ecumenical ferment. However, above all a fact is emerging which is unexpected to many experienced observers: Christians are no longer referring to Christian faith in terms of total exclusiveness; they do not reject the faith, but it is only one of the points of reference for their existence. This is not the wanting 'to serve two masters' that we find in the Gospel, inasmuch as there is no rejection of the authenticity of the value pursued. But it seems as if certain spheres and areas of human experience are proving impenetrable to the quest of faith, and people are always following internal criteria instead. Thus faith is caught up in the crisis of the unity of the human subject.

We have presented this situation with the image of a 'church in fragments', seeking to indicate not only the collective dimension of the phenomenon but also the personal dimension of Christian experience, inasmuch as these two do not seem to have been detached. In fact today the quest for unity, between the churches and within the experience of the believer, is being made in radically different terms from those of the past, when in one way or another everything was under the hegemony of the dimensions of doctrine and discipline.

By choosing the image of the fragment to make this statement, we have wanted to use a metaphor which is open to many meanings. The fragment can be the result of a break, a tear, the remnant of a lost unity. But the fragment can also be a piece that can be fitted into a mosaic without losing its distinctive character, which at the same time produces a unity that is sometimes fascinating: outside itself but not without itself. The fragment evokes resignation, in nostalgia for the past; it is what we have left 'to shore up against our ruin', to use T. S. Eliot's fine expression, quoted in this issue by David Tracy. But fragments of different origin collected in writing or in work can also evoke something that can be reunited and prompt the imagination to reshape different entities, unprecedented figures. At all events, the fragment is never the stone polished by the waves: by itself, even in a pile. And finally, as Panikkar recalls in his contribution, the fragment evokes the broken bread of the Christian eucharist.

The question, after stating the fragmentary form of Christianity and of contemporary Christianity, arises from the very confession of faith by Christians: they believe in one church, as the work of the Spirit. The question is therefore whether this unity has to be the compact and uniform unity of the kind that has often been envisaged and practised by a totalitarian and all-embracing culture, albeit at the cost of serious exclusions. This is not an easy question to answer. In this issue we have sought to offer a series of articles which describe a pattern of reflection rather than offer a solution.

The first part contains contributions which illuminate the present situation. Miklós Tomka describes the historical process as a result of which human experience now presents itself in a fragmented way. He sees this not just as a particularly disturbed phase of the continuum of history but as a planetary historical upheaval. Moreover in his view, in the current fragmentation only a personal decision, without any external support, can allow an integration of experience. Johann Reikerstorf sees the loss of the structuring force of memory and tradition as the main factor which has led to an irreversible crisis in universalism, to the 'episodic' character of our decisions. This necessitates a new paradigm of universality which guarantees the recognition of all human beings. This universality cannot be presupposed as a generality which levels everything out, but must adopt conviviality as a distinctive criterion in order to be capable of recognizing and welcoming the 'otherness' in the other. As if in counterpoint to these analyses, Angelo Maffeis presents the main proposals for church unity developed in contemporary theology: unity as a communion of local churches, in a recovery of the practice of the ancient church; unity in diversity, which leaves the confessional differences intact; unity based on agreement to differ which, in a common recognition of scripture and the creeds of the ancient churches, will tolerate the doctrinal differences that have been asserted in individual churches over time; unity in the service of the world. The diversity of the proposals is in itself an indication of the current difficulties that Christians find in thinking about the ways of unity.

In the second part, which is predominantly historical, the question is addressed to the past of the churches, and is made more precise. Have not the churches in fact always lived in a fragmented condition, beyond affirmations of principle? The question is first raised in the New

Testament canon itself: is that not the basis for a vision of the church in fragments? Hans Dieter Betz, to whom the editors posed the question, formulated in the shadow of a famous article by Ernst Käsemann, gives a discerning reply. In fact he emphasizes how, in the form in which it is asked, the question proves problematical because it begins from the presupposition that there is one church and not already many churches. The ecclesiastical synods which contributed to the formation of the canon between the second and the fourth centuries, while admiring the unity of the church, did not eliminate the plurality of doctrines, rites and forms of church organization and exercise censorship on them, even where there were evidently tensions and oppositions. But the canon as such stands alongside the confessions of faith as an instrument of Christian unity, in a period in which the spread and differentiation of Christianity escaped all institutional control. Betz thus seems to have reservations about the very title of the issue, even if in our view in different terms he grasps the true intention of the question which was put to him.

Again in historical terms, the phenomenon of the fragmentation of Christianity is very complex and cannot be reduced to a single model. Ulrich Körtner presents a 'lost' fragment, which also seems 'threatened': that of Jewish Christianity, a fragment which still continues to pose questions to the churches in the form of contemporary messianic Judaism. Lorenzo Perrone analyses the dynamics of the fragmentation of Eastern Christianity. But he, too, like Körtner, does not fail to consider the present situation, with the prospect of a reconstitution of unity, provided that this is conceived of in a pluralistic and fraternal form. Anne Breton presents the specific form of 'heretical' fragmentation in the mediaeval period. Mediaeval heresy was strictly associated with the conception of a militant church, a conception that produced the spirit of the crusade. The new figure of the heretic arose under the wing of the monastic clergy and chroniclers. For a period closer to us, the seventeenth and eighteenth centuries, Bernard Plongeron introduces us to the complexity of the 'Jansenist' fragment, clarifying its basic intention: to forge an adequate political ethic for a world which was substantially corrupt, whether to refute this world (as happened at Port Royal) or to transform it by injecting into it the ideals of the primitive church (poverty and universal consensus in the election of civil and religious hierarchies).

The historical framework offered here is certainly very limited, but it is useful for understanding the inadequacy of those views which have led to the sometimes violent exclusions of fragments of Christian experience which have not allowed themselves to be integrated into a totalitarian vision of church life. If Nestorius is no longer 'Nestorian', as the joint declaration of the Bishop of Rome and the Patriarch of the Assyrian

Church of the East seems to be saying, though not in those very terms, and if the reciprocal condemnations were the fruit of misunderstanding, then the churches should revise their way of looking at each other from the roots up.

The third part seeks to broaden the problem, setting it within the complexity of the contemporary global horizon. Raimon Panikkar, from an Asian, also Indic, perspective, subjects the view of the unity of the church as an institution to critical analysis: only the view of the church as a living organism and mystery seems to him to be adequate for understanding the 'hurts' and venerating the fragments, as we venerate the 'fragments' of the eucharistic body. From a different perspective, Paulo Suess looks at the way in which 'fragmentation' was introduced into Latin America with the Conquista which, in the name of the universality of European Catholicism, destroyed specific vital projects of the populations of that continent. In his view 'contextuality' can offer the criteria for a counter-offensive which is concerned with the whole life of all, in the shared responsibilities of culturally different social groups. Finally, from a feminist perspective, Lisa Sowle Cahill demonsrates how the emergence of the experience of women in particular shows the limitations of the male point of view, though this has always been presented as universal. The contribution of women to a conception and a praxis of unity is particularly that of the irreducible plurality of vital experiences, of dialogue, of openness to others.

Finally, the fourth part of this issue seeks to offer some positive features for a new understanding of the unity of the churches and of the church. Pierre Vallin offers for discussion the model of 'doctrinal clarity' as a necessary requirement for church life. This model is based on a particular reading of the Council of Trent as progress from the previous 'theological unclarity'. But the history of the church shows greater riches, and the very nature of the church, which appears concretely from this history, cannot be forced into one interpretation. In the current context of the loss of the ancient figure of unity, Jean-Pierre Jossua highlights two approaches: the first is that of a re-creation of unity, in a 'confessing' Christian experience; the second is that of 'partial' identifications, but identifications which for many people represent the greatest possible commitment and not just an attitude of indifference. On the basis of some themes from Newman, the sociology of organized religions and Vatican II, Gregory Baum suggests a pastoral view of the church in which any one office (prophetic, priestly and royal) is corrected by the others; conflicts are not ignored, but at the same time there is a recognition of the work of the Spirit, who performs the *mirabilia Dei* through the mediocrity of the action of the church. By a careful analysis of the concepts of particularity and universality, fragment and form, David Tracy suggests a consideration of catholicity not outside but within and through the particular differences and the fragmentary forms of the church and the whole tradition: for him the fragment above all evokes hope. Johannes Brosseder, confronted with the current refusal of the churches to express the unity which they nevertheless confess as a gift already given in Christ, recalls the need to conceive of unity as communion. This is a communion which Christ himself grants, above all in the liturgy, and which the church should not deny. But for this to happen it is important to abandon the model of organic unity and to substitute for it that of mutual recognition. Joseph Moingt emphasizes how, at the beginning, the unity of the church was one in faith and love, but lacked any organic form and was authoritarian; the unity of the church, conceived as the gathering of all Christians in a centralized institution, is not imposed as such by any law of the gospel and has never existed outside a state of fragmentation. The passion for unity therefore cannot be confused with any kind of political will which leads to the reconstruction of nations or states. Finally, Giuseppe Ruggieri emphasizes the need for fundamental reconsideration, in the content of a culture of otherness, of the significance of the unity which the Spirit works in the churches, as a capacity for relationship and a welcoming of differences.

Giuseppe Ruggieri
Miklós Tomka

I · The Situation

The Fragmentation of Experience in the Modern World

Miklós Tomka

Our experiences of 'yesterday' include the discovery of the world, the unveiling of the laws of nature and the rise of the social sciences. For centuries we have been experiencing humankind increasingly as an entity which can be grasped. The amount of information that we have is increasing vastly. Events from distant regions are communicated to us without any time-lag. We have become participators in a worldwide event. Demographic, technological, cultural, economic and political developments are increasingly accelerating. We are aware of both positive and negative consequences. But the accelerating changes are making us dizzy. We are gradually coming to consider the possibility that our age is not simply a particularly stormy phase in the continuum of history but an upheaval in world history. It is like changing from a mule to an aircraft. Or rather, like the experience of the way in which a balloon can be blown up bigger and bigger and then suddenly bursts into shreds. Conversely, we are witnessing the wonder of a birth, the rise of a new life from chaos.

History is not yet at an end. But it may be that we are now at a break in its course as we have known it.[1] Things do not go on as they used to, but are developing. We can no longer extrapolate the past into the future. Slogans like 'mass society', 'consumer society', 'experience society', 'communication society', 'risk society', are being coined to describe what is special about our present. The modern or even postmodern age has created conditions which are no longer always like the past.[2] The new human condition needs to be analysed thoroughly.

Structural characteristics of the premodern world

In contrast to the present, the past millennia of our history seem almost like a single period. Experiences 'then' were had within narrow chronological, spatial and social horizons. For most people of that time, life was lived within a geographical area which could be easily surveyed. The experiences of merchants, travellers and soldiers could not be communicated widely and at first could not even be checked. There was only modest knowledge of the cosmos, nature and society. A historical consciousness developed in Graeco-Roman or in Jewish-Christian culture; nevertheless, the slow tempo of development created a feeling of immutability and a basic constancy in the situation.

The internal organic unity of pre-industrial society was guaranteed primarily by identical (or at least overlapping) basic principles of organization. A person was at the same time a neighbour, a nephew, a colleague, a member of the church, an authority by virtue of age and a drinking companion. A differentiation of roles and a social organization involving the division of labour came into being without breaking up the unity of experiences. Kinship and local relationships, the organization of work and religious and political structures, existed in the same social framework and essentially consisted of the same people. Since the beginning of human thought, most families had lived in the same place, and thus possessed knowledge going back over generations and personal experience of others. A person's place was predetermined by his or her birth. Generally speaking, individuals could not change themselves or others much. The limited technical and social possibilities restricted possibilities in life – and made it calculable. Opportunities and dangers were relatively easy to recognize. One's relationships with one's fellow men and women were clear, immutable and compulsory. There were almost no alternative careers within the 'normal' system. If one did not want to become asocial, lawless, a vagabond, one had to accept existing conditions. The network of social relations was wide enough to be capable of determining and supervising the whole of life. Its meshes were also narrow enough to be able to offer protection and personal security.

The community which determined the structure of individuals' lives 'from outside' had an equally powerful effect through social relations and the convictions and routines of its culture. Of course the accumulated knowledge that was communicated by tradition was never sufficient to offer answers or explanations on all questions. However, for millennia it forged all aspects of life into a compact unity. The functionality, binding quality and exclusiveness of this one world-view, and a code of behaviour congruent with it, was then endorsed from generation to generation, both cognitively and through social norms. Tradition laid down the limits of thought and behaviour and defined what was real and unreal, permissible and forbidden. The culture taken over from ancestors was communicated and established by a social organization with organic divisions which for its part contributed to the integration and uniformity of the community (society).

However, the permanence and coherence of culture were constantly threatened by the unknown, the unexplained, just as they were challenged by the contradictions and absurdities of life. So an additional support and a final guarantee was needed. This was found in religion, which could incorporate culture into a cosmic and ontological framework, clarify open questions with reference to the supernatural, or stifle them as irrelevant, and oppose meaning to meaninglessness. Thus finally everywhere, according to the same pattern, an interpretation of the world came into being which in principle and *a priori* had an answer to all existing and potential questions and a solution to all conflicts and breaches.[3] The fragmented world of experience was stitched together by religious faith and religious experience. The fragmentation itself was regarded as apparent and incidental. The world was presented as an unbroken totality. Through this contribution religion became the unsurpassable chief guarantor of the cultural and social, and often of the political, system. However, the price it had to pay for that consisted in the instrumental use of religion in uncertainties and contradictions, in breaks in the existing order. God, providence, predestination became causes (not just final but also direct causes) which were used too widely, as a substitute for system-inherent, this-worldly answers and solutions. Religion took on the function of providing order, an explanation and a legitimation in this world: a highly respected role, but nevertheless one in which it filled gaps. It became an irreplaceable and integral part of this world. Of course under such conditions the world could not become an exclusively profane world. Because of the constant direct intervention of the divine it could not completely develop its autonomy, its own inherent wordliness.

The ineffable God of the Old Testament and the 'wholly other' God in Christianity basically resist this profanization. The incarnation bridges the immeasurable distance between God and the world, but without doing away with it. God's infinity and active interest in creation on the one hand and the autonomy of the world on the other continue to be held in a creative tension in Christianity.[4] Or, to be more specific, a complete but idolatry-free worldliness and autonomy of the world only become possible on this basis.[5] In principle, that should make any this-worldly instrumentalizaton of the Christian religion impossible. If praxis did not follow principles, the conclusion had to be that the insight was insufficient, or even that ideas of God were distorted. At all events, the historical evidence that Christianity was often more concerned with the creation and preservation of a cultural and social order which had no contradictions or breaks than with the prophetic distance of Christianity from transitory this-worldly ordinances cannot be disputed. A rootedness in the world led to fundamental inner contradictions. In addition, Christianity was exposed to the protagonists of a secular world. Largely because its role and relevance were fused with its answers and functions in a profane sphere – not only scientific but social and political – the relativization or rejection of its secular positions entailed the relativization of its religious testimony.

The dawn of modernity

A key characteristic of the industrial and bourgeois society that now dawned and, in its wake, of modernity, was the increase of distance in time and space.[6] The horizons of experience and understanding of the world began to extend towards infinity. The great discoveries made the whole globe the sphere of human life. Knowledge and an understanding of reality detached themselves from personal experiences and became autonomous. The sciences became the main agents of modern culture. With universal schooling and the organization of education they became institutions of communication. Technology produced ever more demanding instruments and tools which, because they were used by so many people in so many ways, to some degree took on a life of their own. The economy and politics became autonomous powers which could change the conditions of life and the ordering of society. Consequently, however, they themselves became systems which could be shaped and used, and were identified as the work of human beings. The unity of the pre-modern world was broken up by the perception of a multiplicity.

What we know as the industrial revolution and the rise of bourgeois society; as the creation of a democratic order instead of compulsory systems with a centralistic and hierarchical structure; as colonization and later the independence of great parts of the world; and also as the rapid development of the natural and social sciences, may rightly be termed a unique process of historical differentiation. But it would be wrong to forget how laborious this process was, and what means were used to achieve a unity and continuity in history and culture (of Christian, European origin) despite all the differences. The idea of evolution not only communicated the concept of growth, of enrichment, of the rise of something new, but also asserted a development on the same stem, an uninterrupted connection. Despite all the leaps that were thought possible, a linear logic, a historical teleology was maintained. So the stage of development became a descriptive criterion. Everything could be compared on the continuum of progress. Inter-cultural and other differences could be regarded as different phases.

Ideas about the political order similarly clung to the coherence and interdependence of the world. The discovery of new lands and continents took place under the aegis of Christian missionary efforts, in the framework of the expansion of a dreamed-of single Christian world. Imperialistic thought and a Western claim to hegemony were also behind this. Both the religious and the political frameworks were geographical, just as in their interpretation of history they were 'one-dimensional', following a leading principle. The insight that human destiny was a common one grew with the increase in relations between nations and cultures. Economic collaboration, the international division of labour, the worldwide market, cultural uniformity, reciprocal political dependence, and so on, all demonstrated this link. Now every day it is becoming a more tangible reality. Quite rightly, theories of globalism[7] have come into being, though they can also be used to satisfy an inner existential and emotional need on the part of human beings to have homogeneous conditions to live in, possibilities of mutual understanding, and a more universal, unified view of things.

The apparently neutral approach of the social sciences, especially the concept of social rules and regularities,[8] to some degree leads in the same direction. Whether the guiding mechanisms were seen as a need for integration, rationality, competition, the survival of the fittest brought about by an 'invisible hand', or a striving towards equality (or a combination of these), for the founders of sociology society had its own, pre-indicated way. (Of course the natural sciences – or at least the popularized accounts of them which shaped the thought of a wide public – appealed earlier and more consistently to the recognition of an iron determinism of the material world.)

One of the forefathers of sociology, Auguste Comte, offered a remarkable prognosis in his 'law of three stages'. In his model of evolution he divided the history of the world into three periods. According to Comte, the development led from a magical religious stage to a philosophical revolutionary stage and finally ended in a positive stage. This last phase, the first signs of which Comte thought that he could already see, is characterized by knowledge and the rational manipulation of the laws of nature and society.[9] Though Comte's mechanistic division of time may be inappropriate, he at any rate rightly foresaw and interpreted a tendency of the industrial age which was dawning: the rise of great theories, 'great stories', which hoped to embrace the whole universe, the whole of being. This was the time of the assumption of a determinism in nature and society. It was thought that the law of nature (and natural law) had established that Archimedean point which offered a common denominator not only for understanding and evaluating the world but also for coping with it. Thus human beings hoped to master dead and living matter, to predict the future on the basis of their knowledge, and to be able to use the laws for their own advantage. The divine ordering of the world was replaced by rules and laws which, while cosmic and all-embracing, were nevertheless completely this-worldly. The God who sustains and rules the world was replaced by the human being who controls the laws.

Unstoppable fragmentation: beginnings of a new pluralism

Our present is confronting us with a new situation. For all its cohesion, the world we experience is falling to pieces. Only a few tendencies need to be mentioned: increasing mobility, the way in which the autonomous sub-systems of the social world are becoming independent, the omnipresence of pluralism, and the increasing competition between high cultures which have taken separate courses in history (often named after their different religious traditions).[10]

The most important change in the life of modern men and women consists in the loss of a readiness to take what exists for granted, and in the rise of alternatives. Different and competing worlds have appeared side by side. Formerly, social and geographical mobility were considered to be a movement away from a natural, static, preshaped situation. In our day mobility has become the norm. Education, having a family, work, increasingly call for a change of abode. Demographic pressure and population movements dictated by political and economic factors, and also the desire to travel and other motives, are encouraging a new wave of migration. To change one's abode means to open up new perspectives. Fleeting contacts, like those with neighbours, with the people in the corner shop, or with the postman, are replaced with new ones. By contrast, friendships and other closer human ties are increasingly becoming the object of individual choice and are being detached from geographical proximity. The norms and values of the place and society in which one was born, and practical knowledge of them, are losing their significance. Concrete places and times are becoming staging posts with countless possible continuations. The future of the individual is becoming open.

These changes have transformed human social life. The old communal organization of the social world with its warm nest has been replaced by the impersonal, contractual, formal order of society.[11] The direction of culture, which was formerly regulated by tradition, has primarily been taken over by the individual, who has become autonomous. In connection with this, the internalized convictions of the individual have given way in many places to a dynamic of reflexivity which reacts to the constantly changing environment.[12] Our immediate milieu is increasingly character-ized by multiculturality and by the time-lag in the cultures of the people who live in it. Thus transitoriness and the contingent have become the constitutive characteristics of our everyday culture. Even the space within which people move has changed. It has lost its organic unity and has become segmented, like a mosaic. A single space which can easily be surveyed has become an enchanted castle with many niches which are unequal because they are incalculable; which do not fit together, but constantly change. For a long time politics has been an autonomous sphere of the social system. Soon the economy made itself independent of politics. That is true even within individual states, and even more in the international context. Multinational concerns have often become more powerful than the states in which they are active. Science and technology have developed their own drives and criteria and forms of development. Research centres, universities and industries are autonomous domains. The media have a cultural power which competes with the educational system. And they can only be influenced to a limited degree by governments, a degree which is constantly decreasing. All these and further spheres appeal to their own logic and resist a comprehensive integration. They endorse their independence even over against the citizen. The demands of the system are not the same as that of human well-being.

Citizens are split between the scenes in which their lives take their course. They find security, human warmth, personal acceptance, above all in the family, among relatives, among friends. This private sphere has little in common with the other spheres of their life. They can develop the urge to do things, creative self-realization, achievement, in their professions. A quite different logic controls the public domain, where relations can be made and interests established; where one comes directly into contact with formal social pressures and attempts to master or avoid them. It would be worth considering separately how 'leisure time' has become a sphere of its own, not just for refreshment but also for satisfaction. The definition of 'free' in 'free time' is quite distinctive. In this and other areas one comes upon regularities which legitimate themselves through the constitution of a particular sphere and whose existence is independent of the individual concerned. But one has to observe and follow these rules if one wants to get on in a particular sphere. The sub-systems of society exist to satisfy individual human needs, to institutionalize people's jobs, their income, their development, their information, their entertainment. This 'service of men and women' happens with no reference to values, ethics, religious convictions. If individuals need such things, they can create separate sub-systems for themselves, but they may not apply them in other areas. Many social spheres are resistant to values which are not subordinate to their functioning.

Until recently, an effective common basis for society, an 'anthropological constant', the equality of basic values or something similar, was explicitly or tacitly presupposed. The shift in periods was thus trivialized and stripped of its uniqueness. Today, any general agreement on existential questions seems to have become more than questionable. Individuals (and groups of like-minded individuals) themselves define their relation to the various independent spheres of life and thus their place in the many dimensions of society. They themselves define their identity, differentiating it from other possible options. The shift in the construction of identity to a free choice of values and a relationship which the individual has chosen redefines our world radically (and with it the significance of pluralism; the church; plurality within this society of societies, each with its own intrinsically contingent self-understanding; the relationship between orthodoxy and orthopraxis; the challenges to theology,[13] etc.).

Multiculturalism is a further facet of the same phenomenon. The activity of the missions and the acculturation of the Christian message has been faced with the multiplicity of cultures for many centuries. Historical experience shows that it was possible to disseminate Christianity successfully above all where it came into contact with less developed cultures. It is natural to conclude that it was not so much the content as the packaging and the concomitant circumstances which guaranteed success. Christianity could hardly gain a footing in the high cultures of Asia. These preserved their autonomy, their distance and their resistance to a European Christianity. The isolation which has lasted for centuries is breaking up in our day. India, Japan and China are becoming economic and also cultural partners and competitors. We cannot close our eyes to other interpretations of the world. No group can continue to regard its own tradition as the only one that is right. The formerly strange, exotic cultures appear in one's homeland in the streams of refugees and migrants, and also in the new religious movements. The palette of possible world views and religious positions is becoming increasingly rich. (And the centre of gravity of Christianity – today in the number of members, tomorrow also in the number of students and priests, and the day after perhaps also in the number of readers of theological writings – is inexorably shifting outside Europe and North America.)

Dealing with the fragmentation and incoherence of our experiences

Modern men and women are assailed by experiences which generate tension. They experience the world in its unconditional worldliness, autonomy, differentiatedness, without any inherent connection. And day by day they see their inability to get sufficient grasp and sovereign control of the multiplicity and dynamic of the reality which surrounds them and determines them. Many people break up under the pressure. They include those who have fallen into modernity without any preparation and are suddenly exposed to this tension: those who had previously been shielded from the development by Communism, or the peasants of Africa who are streaming from their tribal alliances into the cities. These experience a cultural shock, the total devaluation of their traditions, the uselessness of almost everything that they have learned. Perhaps even more tragic is the fate of those people who, having been brought up in highly developed industrial countries, must come to the realization that their aspirations and possibilities are irreconcilable.

Modernity is producing more 'drop-outs', more failed people, than any previous society, simply because the fragmentation and the complicated interconnection of the conditions that have to be coped with transcends anything previously experienced. The increase in the number of those who have been stranded can easily be followed in the statistics of the religious welfare organizations and those organizations which deal with nervous conditions.

The fragmentary experience of life can prompt three different answers: suppression, rejection, and acceptance of the modern condition. Suppression means not bothering, playing down the problems. The media and the trivialization to which they contribute make an important contribution here. Global problems, catastrophes, fundamental contradictions, threats to our earth, are being remodelled as entertainment. The whole world is brought into one's room, but mixed up with games and fantasies, and thus is robbed of any reality that can be shaped. It becomes a playground outside one's own sphere of action. Human beings are merely onlookers. We know that our world is contingent, that events can take place in different ways, but this knowledge has no personal consequences. Helplessness produces fatalism. It worked somehow yesterday; why should it not go on working tomorrow? People no longer believe what they are told. In practice they are familiar with statistical probability, e.g. that the technology around us will not fail. They often trust the scientists to know better. They trust the new priestly caste of the specialists. They regard everyday life with a particularly high degree of trust.[14] Attempts are made to keep basic differences of opinion under control by pragmatic rules, by formalization.[15] Routine becomes a sacred cow, because there is nothing else that (or Who) is holy to anyone.

This rejection is on many levels. A large number of people attempt to overcome the divides in the modern world by setting up private idols. One's own person, power, professional career, sex and enjoyment become centres to which everything is related. Others simply stop wanting to join in. People can increasingly give up bothering about their own affairs and thus also the possibility of having a say and helping to determine the situation, the more autonomous and differentiated the institutional systems which concern them have become: more and more complex because of their own intrinsic needs. Many people are specialists in nothing, some perhaps in one or two areas. But since they are not experts, no one asks them, nor can they have a say. Their functionally limited activity is needed, but not their persons. So they withdraw from politics, from all organizations and from public life generally, into the private sphere. They do not become members of a party or trade union, or they cease to renew their membership. They no longer vote. They no longer use the local public forums. They become merely consumers. They therefore lose interest in the way in which individual areas and the whole of public life (including the church) function. They capitulate to the complexity and sheer magnitude of their world. Instead of taking an active part, they have the impression that everyone is getting at them. Soon their participation consists only in using the achievements of the spheres mentioned, and in offering an inconsequential criticism of the 'half-baked methods of politics', 'the spokesmen of the economy', 'the stupidity of the media' and so on. Because they are forced to, they take note of the autonomy of the individual spheres of life (or relevant institutions) which are independent of them, which they cannot influence, and make these the basis of their action. But inwardly disillusioned, they withdraw into private life.

This withdrawal can also come about in the social dimension. One's own culture or one's own group can be declared an idol. Because the absolute pre-eminence of one's own society, one's own institution, one's own faith, is not accepted by the world, attempts are made to isolate them from the vast undifferentiatedness of pluralistic society and develop a counter-world. In this enterprise a counter-culture is established just for one's own use. This does not put the state and the order of modernity in question, but simply seeks to keep it at bay. No attempt is made to make one's own, possibly critical, contribution towards shaping the world. In this way conflicts are removed. The collapse of society into sub-systems is almost endorsed by this tendency. So this enterprise can easily reckon with some success. At the end of the nineteenth and beginning of the twentieth century, in many European countries the Catholic Church opted for institutional separation, in order to be able to preserve and cultivate its character undisturbed. There can be attempts at a similar strategy here and there, though because of world-wide communication and mobility it is increasingly difficult to maintain isolation in modern society.

There is an aggressive variant of separation. An attempt can be made to fight for a higher status for one's own cultures or one's own group at the cost of others, by force. Differentiation, pluralism, the freedom of the individual, can be opposed by historically rooted nostalgias and the interests of a group which is identified ethnically, linguistically or in some other way. The multiplicity of modernity, felt as a threat, can thus become a source of an egotistic and bitter nationalism. In the hope of gaining undivided unity and a timelessness of immutability for one's own culture, if need be, a fight will be engaged in with the whole world. Thus an anachronistic group egotism may explain the attractiveness of modern totalitarianisms and nationalistic civil wars.

The unbounded over-valuation of one's own convictions can also lead to egocentricity. Everything else is intransigently rejected. Even members of one's own culture, one's own community, who engage in conversations with those who think differently are avoided. An attempt is made to exclude them, or one withdraws from them. On the basis of the one and undivisible truth which their community claims to possess, a group of the 'pure' can form. That is how sects come into being. In another variant, reflection on one's roots is made the aim. The allegedly unitary, undifferentiated foundations, with no period or context, which can only be interpreted in one way, are conjured up in face of the fragmentation, multiplicity and contingent experience of modernity. Fundamentalisms come into being in politics, in and outside the churches.[16]

The third possible existential response to the incoherence and fragmentation of experience is to affirm it while at the same time creating one's own individual harmony. This calls for a three-level position. First, an acceptance of the autonomy of the individual spheres of life and an attempt to come to terms with them while respecting them. Secondly, a recognition that the world as a whole is in pieces, and no longer has a comprehensive structural principle. Moreover it is still caught up in a rapid and contingent change to pluralism, and has therefore long since ceased to be calculable. Thirdly, however, there is need for a conviciton that the differentiaton of the world does not destroy the possibility of ordering the individual scenes of life into a single system from a personal standpoint. Human beings are virtually forced to this integration by their psyches[17] and the need to simplify everyday action. Finally, it is by no means impossible to formulate all spheres of life in terms of personal, moral or other expectations. One can keep one's integrity, even though it is becoming increasingly impossible to survey one's environment. One can lay down one's own values and criteria as a standard for one's behaviour. In addition, a decision is needed, which can be made by no one but the person concerned, who must be aware of the transitoriness of this decision. The more complex and vast the environment, and the more honestly held competing options exist in the same social sphere, the more contingent a person's own choice becomes.

This choice can be supported and safeguarded by the testimony of others, and by a sense of being addressed; in other words by relationships. But it will no longer be a pre-existing, compelling necessity which follows from a creation that has become impersonal and unapproachable in its complexity, or from a culture and society which have been reified (and perhaps as a result have become a source of alienation). Accordingly, the fragmentation of experience can no longer be completely bridged in the cognitive sphere; however, it can be given a supportive framework in interpersonal[18] relationships, and also in the relationship between God and his image on earth. Yet it has to be said once again that these relationships do not exist of themselves, *a priori*, but must be created by personal decisions.

One's own position can come up against the resistance of the system. One's own preferences need not always and automatically coincide with the wishes and expectations of others. One has to live with this multiplicity. Establishing one's own convictions may involve struggles, struggles against the logic of the system and against efforts by fellow human beings which go in another direction. One will probably not always emerge completely as the victor from these struggles. Thus modernity is the time of freedom, of alternatives, of pressure to make a decision,[19] of competition, and of compromise. The fragmentation of experience can be overcome only by those who are capable of making decisions.

Translated by John Bowden

Bibliography

1. Francis Fukuyama, *The End of History and the Last Man*, Harmondsworth 1992.
2. From a bibliography which is almost unmanageable I shall mention just two landmarks: Jean François Lyotard, *The Postmodern Condition*, Manchester 1984; Wolfgang Welsch, *Unserer postmoderne Moderne*, Weiheim 1991.
3. Peter L. Berger, *The Sacred Canopy. Elements of a Sociological Theory of Religion*, Garden City 1967.
4. Karl Rahner, 'Theological Reflections upon the Problem of Secularization', in *Theological Investigations* 10, New York and London 1973, 318–48.
5. Johann-Baptist Metz, *Zur Theologie der Welt*, Mainz and Munich 1968, esp. p. 42.
6. Anthony Giddens, *The Consequences of Modernity*, Oxford 1990.
7. Mike Featherstone (ed.), *Global Culture. Nationalism, Globalization and Modernity*, London 1990; Roland Robertson, *Globalization. Social Theory and Global Culture*, London 1992.

8. Martin Hollis, *The Philosophy of Social Science*, Cambridge 1994.
9. Auguste Comte, *Cours de philosophie positive* I–VI, Paris 1839–42.
10. Samuel P. Huntington, 'The Clash of Civilizations?', *Foreign Affairs* 72, 1993/3, 22–49.
11. Ferdinand Tönnies, *Gemeinschaft und Gesellschaft* (1887), Darmstadt 1972.
12. An early account which became a bestseller was David Riesman et al, *The Lonely Crowd. A Study of the Changing American Character*, New Haven 1950.
13. Joachim Mehlhausen (ed.), *Pluralismus und Identität*, Gütersloh 1995.
14. Giddens, *The Consequences of Modernity* (n. 6) and Niklas Luhmann, *Vertrauen*, Stuttgart 1968.
15. Niklas Luhmann, *Legitimation durch Verfahren*, Neuwied 1969.
16. Some especially well-known works on the topic are: Gilles Keppel, *Le Revanche de Dieu. Chrétiens, juifs et musulmans à la reconquête du monde*, Paris 1991; Hermann Kochanek (ed.), *Die verdrängte Freiheit. Fundamentalismus in den Kirchen*, Freiburg 1991; Paul Ladrière and René Luneau (eds), *Le retour des certitudes. Évenements et orthodoxie depuis Vatican II*, Paris 1987; Martin E. Marty and R. Scott Appleby (eds), *Fundamentalism Observed*, Chicago 1991 (and subsequent volumes).
17. Leon Festinger, *A Theory of Cognitive Dissonance*, New York 1957.
18. Martin Buber, *Das Dialogische Prinzip*, Heidelberg 1962.
19. Peter L. Berger, *The Heretical Imperative. Contemporary Possibilities of Religious Affirmation*, New York and London 1979.

The God of Christians and the Fragmentation of the Postmodern World

Johann Reikerstorfer

Christian faith with its talk of God does not remain unaffected by the processes of fragmentation in the world in which we live. That makes its situation precarious. At all events, talk of the God of Christianity brings in the problem and topic of universality. The God of Christians is either a God for all men and women, or not a God at all. God is only 'my' God if God can also be the God of others. That raises the question whether Christian faith is in fact just one experience among others, just one experience of meaning and form of life among others – without any normative nucleus, i.e. without any claim to truth. The following reflections take up theological suggestions by J. B. Metz and seek to express and take further in connection with our question the basic category of the *memoria passionis* which he has developed, as the criterion of truth and universality.[1]

I. The new situation: an attempt at a description

1. The disintegration of the myth of modernity

Since the European Enlightenment, Christianity has experienced the fate of a particular social existence. Faith has forfeited its previously unbroken acceptance by society; it has become marginal and has largely been driven into a private sphere which is socially irrelevant. Enlightened consciousness also interpreted its secular strength in terms of criticism of traditional religion. It deciphered religion as a compensatory phenomenon, without being aware of how much in adopting this approach it was still standing on the ground of the tradition which it criticized. This generated the myth of modernity, which with its unshaken basic assumptions came to determine the social consciousness. However, myths are influential only until they are put in question.

Meanwhile this myth itself is now in crisis. The crisis indicates a deep-seated change of mentality. It has long since reached the foundations of our social and cultural awareness, and in so doing has produced a sense of being at the limits of modernity ('postmodernity'). The processes of individualization have been taken so far that they are distorting and destroying the unity of social life; in the fragmentation of spheres of life, the growing diffusion and sheer vastness and complexity of the new scene, it has become more difficult to get any bearings.

With its ideals of reason, freedom and coming of age, the 'strong' I of modern times which is enciphered in the myth of modernity is proving to be an exaggeration, an illusion or a lie. It is giving way to a 'plural' I which transforms its attitudes into flexible options, an I to which the prospect of unity and totality seems totally illusory. The postmodern consciousness and the postmodern sense of life move unpretentiously within narrow perspectives; unmoved and without feeling much of a loss, the postmodern consciousness has left global solutions, total claims and answers behind in favour of the multiplicity, the differentiatedness and the plurality of possible experiences and standpoints. Standpoints are adopted until they are proved untenable. Decisions are no longer made in the long term, but to some degree with a built-in option to change them; commitments are much more scattered than before, and life-style is becoming 'episodic'.

R. Musil gave an impressive illustration of this collective change of mentality in his novel *The Man without Properties*. Like Nietzsche, he too anticipates much of the postmodern mood. He regrets the 'hypothetical' lifestyle of his time as a manifestation of the 'possibility person', who on the one hand becomes the advocate of creative ideas which are not yet born, and on the other loses his determination in the chaos of possibilities. Ulrich, the hero of the novel – significantly, he is said originally to have been called Anders ('Other') – inevitably regards any definitive commitment, any finality in time, in short any fixed character, as a 'straitjacket', and rejects it. His house, which contains objects of very different styles, reflects a freedom which can always be 'different' – different, moreover, with reference to the nominalist idea of God as 'unmotivated' omnipotence. It is also said of him that he was a believing person who merely did not believe anything. Luther's well-known saying, 'Here I stand, I can do no other', has undergone a remarkable change. It has become 'Here I stand, I can also do otherwise.' Is this just a literary fiction or the sense of a simmering identity crisis for the modern subject?[2]

2. *The limits and crisis of universalism*

To clarify this change in consciousness it is important to look at the crisis of universalism which is linked with it. In the public presentation of the mass media the face of the other has become vaguer, more abstract, less of a presence.[3] And this has happened although more than ever, day by day we are confronted with information about others, about their fates, their-sufferings and their destruction. Evidently it lies in the very nature of communication through the media that the way in which they present things makes 'the other' simply others who are a matter of indifference, who are superfluous and can be replaced. The social sphere is absorbed aesthetically; the reduction of the other to superficiality is technologically guaranteed in the 'telecity'. Must not such a presentation which increasingly blurs the other have an effect on those to whom it is made? And will not this loss of 'otherness' in the social world also have effects on the moral determination of freedom, which is achieved only in the challenge from others? If memory and moral responsibility are intrinsically linked, then to forget the other inexorably threatens the universalism of morality with its universalistic options. Common links, which previously contributed to social life, become more fragile; this is one reason why the extremely individualized worlds in which people live remain endangered by new outbreaks of violence.

Against the background of these experiences the question of the presuppositions of the great myth of modernity becomes unavoidable. The process of secularization could initially still presuppose a certain degree of cultural coherence on the basis of effective elements of tradition which were taken for granted. Partialization lived by the universalism of a religious tradition, opposed by an emancipatory society which supposed that it had no presuppositions. By contrast, late modern pluralism sees itself confronted with a situation in which human beings must themselves produce the moral and social conditions of their existence, since memory and tradition have meanwhile lost their structuring force. In this loss, it seems that the resistance of modern men and women is disappearing when faced with all the dangers to and divisions of its subjective identity in the turbulences of its world.

Theoreticians of modernity describe this situation as that stage of modernity in which it becomes aware of its risk. 'Reflexive' democracy is aware that, after tradition, it is in crisis over its foundations, and this comes through in politics as uncertainty.[4] New decisionisms emerge. Or uncertainty becomes long-term and can only be controlled by discourse.

Such phenomena of crisis stand in a strange and striking contrast to the new challenges and tasks of globalization, which aims at one world society. Will it and can it succeed as a multicultural concept? Or does it not remain a fate which can be experienced, which must continually become the flashpoint for conflicts over civilization and culture? And quite centrally, can it succeed in the medium of a strictly formal, purely procedural, reationality of discourse *à la* Habermas, once the offer of contextualized uniformity is increasingly losing its power to orientate praxis?

Does not a crisis of the modern subject itself underlie the postmodern-pluralistic form of consciousness, a crisis which has its roots in the loss of a universalism of binding social factors with a religious foundation? The problem is not the Enlightenment as such. The problem is rather that – presumably under the influence of the Christian tradition, which was still not totally quenched – modernity still continued to define human beings with strong categories, that it was not yet aware of human fragility, since on the fundamental premises of human equality it regarded human dignity as inviolable. It forgot to safeguard and anchor its practical knowledge (reason which seeks freedom and justice) in traditions which make freedom possible and guide it. It is this that makes the so-called 'project' of modernity itself prone to crisis, and on the other hand explains its increasing need for praxis-orientating, formative and structuring horizons of meaning. The problem of recognizing others becomes the question of a concrete, historical ethos, which in today's conditions can be regarded as being capable of universalization. In the confrontation of various cultural worlds, this possibility of universalization would inevitably need to result in the formation of a criterion of 'conviviality' to direct the internal and external discussion about culture, if the clash of civilizations predicted by S. P. Huntington is to be overcome. In the end, the perception of others is decisive for the humanity of human beings and the humane character of a culture.

II. Christianity in the crisis of universalism

Now Christianity, too, with its universalistic offers of meaning, is finding itself in crisis in these social processes of fragmentation. These processes not only weaken men and women today, but are also an attack on the potential of biblical universalism and its visions which further humanity. The decline in a capacity to remember and the spread of amnesia in our late modern societies are making this God of history, promise and judgment fade away. The biblical remembrance of God in 'memory' of the others, the oppressed and injured others, is drawn into the undertow of a 'psychologizing', 'aestheticizing' retreat from historical responsibility. Religion which serves the quest for the whole, unirritable, I which is the result of success in finding identity, deteriorates to become a phenomenon of immunization, assuagement and unburdening. And with the loss of a global horizon, it is threatened with the fate of godlessness. This identity crisis for biblical faith then inevitably also has effects on its relationship to society, to culture as a whole. A postmodern religiosity with a natural mythical tone also migrates to the periphery of society, and cannot be a *critical* accompaniment to its humanization.

Only in a new attentiveness to the other can Christianity regain the question of God as the question of humanity. Fragmentation and pluralism do not make such attentiveness *a priori* impossible. The end of universalist concepts, the perceived emptiness of abstract claims to totality and their demonopolization, and the untenability of a universally binding ethical code to regulate social life, are also new opportunities for a humane culture. The current pluralistic situation does not offer a solution, but poses a problem of assimilation, i.e. of shaping. For to deal with pluralism and fragmentation in full awareness of the problem does not mean conforming with pluralism, nor does it mean denying or undermining the pluralism of cultural worlds. Rather, it means finding a criterion for dealing with pluralism and fragmentation from particular cultural perspectives in a way which can command a consensus. We shall have to discuss this in the concluding fourth section.

III. Christianity in the pluralism of the religions

Peter Berger has described the relationship of Christianity within religious pluralism by the three theological responses of 'exclusivism', 'inclusivism' and 'pluralism'.[5] 'Exclusivism' distances and depotentiates the historical religions in the name of the divine revelation (see Barth). Its distinction between faith and religion is fatal, because it suggests the notion of a pure Christianity which anxiously immunizes itself from all forms of religion. Its decisionism excludes the religious question of truth and also makes Christianity incapable of self-criticism.

By contrast, 'inclusivism' recognizes the significance of other religions for salvation. It interprets them as 'implicit' or 'anonymous' Christianity (see Rahner). But with this interpretation it undermines the historical self-understanding of the non-Christian religions, commandeers it and finally makes itself incapable of receiving their prophecy.

By contrast, the religious theory of 'pluralism' recognizes the multiplicity of religious traditions and attributes authenticity to them as phenomena by seeing them as perspectival manifestations of a divine reality. According to John Hick, this 'noumenal' reality makes itself known as a phenomenon in the redemptive transformation of the self-centredness of human existence into centredness on this Unconditional (Real) itself. However, right from the start this thesis of a pluralistic theology of religion has abdicated from the religious truth-question; it regards any claim to the truth as dangerous or obsolete, so that it does not even need to make such a claim any more. It is probably to be understood as a reaction to a 'rational' interpretation of religion which not only conceals its own origin in Christianity but also pretends to universality – at the expense of the historical religions and the way in which they present themselves. Religious identity cannot be spoken of in historical-narrative terms in the garb of a universal concept of religion.

Is there a criterion for proving and recognizing religious identity and authenticity which can take us beyond the relativism of a religious pluralism? If we have to begin from the way in which the loss of tradition that can be observed in Western societies affects and challenges not only Christianity, but to an increasing degree all the great traditions, the question of such a criterion for inter-religious encounter as well is clearly an urgent one. How, and on what basis, can these religions come to an understanding with one another in the conflicts which threaten culture and civilization? Is the offer of our hermeneutics of religion enough for such a religious dialogue, if in the general threat to religious identities it is concerned with their significance as bringing salvation, rather than merely seeing them as enterprises orientated on understanding? What is sought is a new paradigm of universality which does not exclude the other religions (exclusivism), does not engage in theological imperialism (inclusivism), and does not make them disappear in a relativistic pluralism of religions.

IV. A new paradigm of universality?

'Postmodernity' is an ambivalent phenomenon. It sees through the abstractedness and totalitarian tendencies of great ideas, great subjects and stories (see J. F. Lyotard); it destroys universalisms which have forgotten otherness and regards universalist claims which issue in a colonialist and expansionist domination of others as obsolete. Nevertheless, the new awareness of difference and plurality can be seen as an opportunity for a new understanding of universality and universalizing. Universality is not an irritating uniformity, nor is it a generality which brings everything down to the same level. It is the recognition of the different, unequal, 'other', other. In contrast to all suggestions of equality, it communicates itself through non-identity. It is a 'subject' with the other only in the recognition of the other's history, which ultimately proves to be that other's history in 'passion'. A paradigm of universality with this orientation could at least be understood as a corrective to abstract universalisms of reason, as they have been produced with ever greater frequency since the Enlightenment and in its wake. As J. B. Metz has pointed out,[6] it is rooted in the *memoria passionis* as a form of respect for the suffering of others which marks out all the great religions and cultures. Such a universalization, which strives for the language of negativity under post-traditional conditions, would also be in search of the God who has bound his promises to the memory of the suffering other. To take seriously the recollection of suffering opens up a promising perspective for Christian talk of God in an age of postmodern fragmentations. It may then become a public pointer to the topic of God which does not fall silent in the age of plurality and difference. In this ecumene, an ecumene of empathy, the great religions could also come closer to each other and play a productive part in shaping a world society.

Translated by John Bowden

Notes

1. Cf. now J. B. Metz, 'Im Eingedenken fremden Leids. Zu einer Basiskategorie christlicher Gottesrede', in id., J. Reikerstorfer and J. Werbick, *Gottesrede*, Münster 1996.

2. See M. Foucault's talk of the death of the subject with reference to Nietzsche's vision of the 'farewell to the human being', in id., *Archäologie des Wissens*, Frankfurt 1973.

3. Cf. *Concilium* 1993/6, *Mass Media*.

4. See the basic text by J. B. Metz, 'Politik und Religion auf dem Boden der Moderne', in H. J. Höhn (ed.), *Krise der Immanenz. Religion am Ende der Moderne*, Frankfurt 1995, 265–79.

5. P. Berger, *Sehnsucht nach Sinn. Glauben in einer Zeit der Leichtgläubigkeit*, Frankfurt and New York 1994. For information on the state of the discussion see R. Schwager (ed.), *Christus allein? Der Streit um die pluralistische Religionstheologie*, WD 160, Freiburg 1996.

6. Metz's remark on the 'authority' of the suffering is an apt one: 'It cannot be prepared for hermeneutically or be safeguarded in discourse. It is preceded by the obedience of understanding – at the cost of any morality. This authority cannot even be discussed; where it is concerned, morality cannot even refuse to give an order, perhaps with a reference to "autonomy". In this sense the encounter with the suffering of others is a kind of "exceptional state", for which there are no more general rules, to which one could refer – with provisos' (id., 'Im Eingedenken fremden Leids' [n. 1]).

Current Theological Discussion on the Unity of the Church

Angelo Maffeis

The history of ecclesiology is one of the areas in which the close connection between church life and theological reflection is most evident. Like the majority of the questions which have been to the forefront of theology in different periods of history, reflection on the unity of the church and its criteria has always developed in relation to concrete problems which for the most part were presented as threats to the integrity or the cohesion of the church community. The novel feature of the contemporary context, compared with past times, is the birth and consolidation of the ecumenical movement. Reflection on unity today therefore generally presupposes a concern to overcome the obstacles which stand in the way of full communion between the various churches and seeks further reconciliation. While participation in the ecumenical movement bears witness to the presence in all the churches of a common will to promote unity, from the first encounters between the different ecclesial traditions it has proved that ways of achieving the unity of the church have been envisaged quite differently. Nor should this seem surprising, given that the content of unity is defined within a particular ecclesiology, and the very conception of the church is one of the main themes on which ecumenical dialogue seeks a consensus. Beyond the specific sphere of interconfessional dialogue, if we look at the general theological panorama, we can see that the reflection on unity carried on within confessional theologies has been characterized by a greater attention to the wider ecumenical horizon.

From the beginning of the century, the reflection carried on in the dialogue between confessional theologies and in ecumenical encounters has been accompanied by a Leitmotif: the unity sought must not be understood as uniformity and levelling out, but as a unity in plurality. In particular, it does not call for a centralized structure. However, in fact it seems that many protagonists of the ecumenical movement have the conviction that the majority of current differences in the churches must be overcome because they are incompatible with the unity sought.

This presupposition – sometimes explicit, but more often tacit – is now increasingly being put in question. There are various reasons for this. From a theological perspective, the dialogues which have been carried on reveal the existence of an irreducible nucleus of diversity in the historical forms taken by Christian faith and church life, differences which often relate to experiences and 'forms of thought' that are difficult to integrate. It is no coincidence that today we are seeing the revival of the category of 'fundamental' difference which originated in the nineteenth century, in the context of the discussion aimed at identifying the fundamental point of difference between Catholics and Protestants. In addition to the theological element, a cultural factor is also contributing towards determining this new sensitivity to difference. The 'postmodern' mentality has made theology, too, more diffident about the possibility of developing a rational and all-embracing scheme which can state the whole of revelation adequately. This is inevitably reflected, for example, in the understanding of the criterion of orthodoxy, which has traditionally been used as the privileged instrument for tracing the boundaries of church unity.

In this article I intend to examine the way in which contemporary theology conceives of the unity of the church. The perspective which I shall assume in reading the theological debate is indicated in the title of this issue. So I shall attempt to focus in particular on the relationship between the reality of the church as encountered by the believer, the way in which it identifies itself in the place where that believer lives, and the wider, universal unity of believers, with the different forms and structures in which such unity is realized. I shall present schematically some models on the basis of which this relationship is conceived, pointing by way of example to some writers and documents which have given a particularly clear formulation of these models. Finally, I shall seek to bring out the strong points and limits of the models, along with the questions that they pose to theological reflection.

Unity as communion of local churches

A first quite significant thread in contemporary reflection on the church is that which aims to recover the ecclesiology of the ancient church. In this way an attempt is made in particular to overcome the universalistic vision which, since the Gregorian Reform in the eleventh century, has made it impossible in the West to produce a true theology of the local church, since the whole reality of the church has tended to be absorbed into the universal church with the pope at its head. The recovery of the ecclesiological conceptions of the first millennium has made it possible to rediscover catholicity not only as a property of the universal church, but as an original mark of the local church, in which the elements which give the church existence are present. This catholicity must therefore be first of all thought of as the fullness of the mystery of salvation which is communicated, received, celebrated and witnessed to by the Christian community in a concrete place. In the local church is made present the original and sole reality of the apostolic church, and the eucharist celebrated by it represents the culmination of the expression of the church in one place. From this centre, the local reality of the church is also extended into other areas of life, having to incarnate itself within a cultural context and take on elements which allow the Christian message to be expressed in a significant way.[1] In this perspective the concept of communion/*koinonia* becomes a basic ecclesiological category. It makes possible a description of the reality of the church in its local dimension as the fruit of the communion which comes from above and as a communal experience of those who make up the church. At the same time the category of communion also makes it possible to reflect the relationship between the local churches which recognize one another as participants in the one mystery of salvation and which therefore establish a network of 'synodical' communication among themselves, in order to demonstrate the bond of communion which unites them.

This theological view is present in the most recent texts of Faith and Order and has also been used to describe the objective pursued by the World Council of Churches. The Declaration on Unity made at the 1991 Canberra Assembly pointed out that the unity of the church to which Christians are called is a *koinonia* given and expressed in the common confession of the apostolic faith, in a common sacramental life which begins with the one baptism and is celebrated communally in the one eucharistic communion, a common life in which members and ministers are reciprocally recognized and reconciled in a common mission which bears witness to the gospel of the grace of God to all and which serves the whole creation. The objective of the quest for full communion is achieved when all the churches are able to recognize in one another the one, holy, catholic and apostolic church in its fullness. This full communion will be expressed at the local and universal level through conciliar forms of life and action. The churches are bound together by this communion in all the aspects of their life: in confessing the one faith and in commitment to it in worship and testimony, in decision and in action.[2]

Fundamental to this conception of unity is a reciprocal recognition on the part of local churches which takes place on the basis of a criterion of homogeneity. This criterion functions in two ways: first, the local church is authentic when elements of the apostolic church can be recognized as being present in it; and secondly, the universal communion of the local churches is present when each one of them recognizes in the others the essential elements of the church and can therefore communicate with them. The shared celebration of the eucharist therefore represents not only the summit of the life of the local church but also the manifestation of the universal communion between the churches.

Unity through diversity

The ideal framework evoked by the notion of *koinonia* often comes up against a reality in which the differences between the churches are so deep that they hinder their full reciprocal recognition as local churches, incarnating the one apostolic church in different spheres and cultures. The noting of differences which resist any theological effort at consensus has prompted the development of an alternative conception of unity which regards the confessional differences as a permanent element that cannot be overcome. The principle of the legitimacy of confessional differences within the unity of the church has been put forward in different versions which have more or less emphasized the reconciliation needed between the differences, or the possibility that they will continue in their present form. However, one common feature of these suggestions is a critical attitude towards the course of ecumenical dialogue as it has been pursued so far.

Adopting this line, Oscar Cullmann has put forward the view that what characterizes the different confessional traditions is an expression of the charisms aroused by the Spirit, each of which contributes to unity. This unity must therefore be thought of as a unity through difference. The universal church must therefore be thought of as a 'communion of churches peacefully separate' (or 'autonomous', according to the most recent formulation, which has been introduced in order to avoid misunderstandings), in which the different charisms aroused by the Spirit remain each with its own physiognomy, and there is no attempt to unify them or assimilate them to one another. Not every separation is necessarily the consequence of sin, and despite their division, the present-day churches have proved a powerful stimulus for avoiding distortions of their own charisms.[3]

Here the particularity of ecclesial reality is seen in a confessional sense, with a tendency, at least in some cases, to identify it in a quite undifferentiated way with a gift of the Spirit. The way in which the universal unity between confessionally separate churches is manifested is created through dialogue, understood as a process of continuous exchange between subjects who must maintain their differences. So the dialogue is not aimed at a consensus which eliminates diversity; it cannot be regarded as an imperfect realization of communion but represents the very form of church unity.[4]

A differentiated unity in the profession of faith

The recognition of the legitimacy of the formal differences with which the separated churches exist today puts in question one of the fundamental criteria to which church history bears witness: church unity is based on agreement in the profession of faith. There is no doubt that the understanding of the significance and the extension of unity in the profession of faith has undergone profound changes. Today there is a clearer awareness of the distance between the reality that is believed and the doctrinal formulation in which this belief finds expression, and of the varied relationship between the truths of faith and the centre of the Christian revelation (cf. the principle of the 'hierarchy of truths' formulated in *Unitatis redintegratio* 11). With the intention of indicating a practicable way towards church unity, H. Fries and K. Rahner have proposed a conception of unity in faith based on the acceptance of the fundamental Christian truths enunciated in scripture, the Apostles' Creed and the creeds of Nicaea and Constantinople; there must be a 'gnoseo-logical tolerance' of the other doctrines put forward by the churches.[5] This means that in no particular church may a proposition which in any other particular church is a binding dogma be rejected decisively and in confessional terms. Furthermore, however, going beyond the demand that scripture and the ancient creeds be accepted, no particular church may be required to make an express and positive confession of faith in a dogma of another church; this must await a wider consensus in the future. In connection with this principle, the current practices of every church towards and with its members are to be maintained.[6]

Abstention from judgment on the contrasting truth-claims put forward by different doctrines is legitimate in a cultural situation in which the majority of believers find it almost impossible to understand the reasons for the doctrinal controversies of the past. If within the Catholic Church not every Christian is asked to give explicit assent to every single proposition taught by the magisterium, on the basis of the same principle it is possible to think of a unity of the churches now separated, provided that none of them declares that a proposition regarded as absolutely binding by another church cannot be reconciled in an absolute and positive way with its own understanding of the faith. Whereas in the past there were absolute oppositions, today it can be doubted whether they still exist with the same absoluteness. In fact, if theological dialogue between the churches has not achieved complete consensus, certainly it has created a situation in which it is no longer legitimately possible to consider an opposing doctrine as being in radical contradiction with the fundamental substance of the Christian faith.

The intention underlying the proposals made by Fries and Rahner seems to make possible a union of the churches based on a differentiated agreement in the profession of the faith. This agreement must be explicit and complete as far as the central nucleus of the Christian revelation is concerned, witnessed to by scripture and formulated in the creeds of the ancient church. However, differences may be tolerated over the specific doctrinal forms that the Christian faith has taken in time and which can be presented in a reciprocal contrast. Once the explicit contrast in the form of condemnations has been overcome, the deep intention of the doctrinal formulations, orientated on the centre of the Christian revelation, makes it possible to accept them in their diversity, each in its own perspective. A corrective which has rightly been suggested to the proposals of Fries and Rahner is to transform abstention from judgment into a positive judgment of compatibility.

Unity in service to the world

The criticism directed at the ecumenical method which hinges on the quest for theological consensus as a condition for ecclesial communion has in some cases resulted in the rejection of a church unity conceived primarily in terms of confessions of faith or ecclesial structures, giving the decisive role to the service rendered by the church in the world. It is argued that in fact this is the only way in which it is possible to maintain the necessary link between the unity of the churches and the unity of humankind.

According to Konrad Raiser, a paradigm shift is taking place in the contemporary ecumenical movement. The classical paradigm, character-ized by christocentricity and concentration on the church understood as the sacrament of Christ, is proving increasingly inadequate. However, a new paradigm is developing which stems from a trinitarian understanding of God and the relationship between God, the world and humankind. It sees life, understood as a network of multiple relationships, as a central point of reference and thinks of the church as a communion which brings about a relationship between differences. The basic category which takes on the function of a unifying element in the new paradigm is no longer that of history, but that of relationship.[7] In this way it is possible to restore its original meaning to the concept of ecumene: it refers to the whole inhabited earth, to a totality understood not in the abstract but as the whole of vital relations. So ecumenical commitment cannot be limited to a quest for unity between Christians, but also includes dialogue with other religions. Its aim is not just to bring about the unity of the church but also to contribute towards making the earth habitable. In this way the pledge for justice and peace ceases to be an expression of Christian responsibility in the particular sphere of social and political life and is put at the very centre of the confession of faith and church life. The main importance attributed to this aspect of Christian action elevates orthopraxy to being the decisive criterion for the existence of the church and its unity, while it tends to relativize the traditional 'intra-ecclesial' criteria of unity in the faith, in the sacraments and in ministerial structure.

In many ways this reflection can be regarded as the theoretical expression of the experience of the conciliar process on justice, peace and the preservation of creation. It is confirmed by the document *Costly Unity*, which brings together the results of a 1993 World Council of Churches consultation.[8] The text asserts the need to connect the concilar process for a commitment to justice, peace and the preservation of creation launched at the Sixth General Assembly of the WCC in Vancouver in 1983 with the dialogue on church unity carried on by Faith and Order. It points out that the essence of the church is involved in the process of justice, peace and the preservation of creation. It is not enough to assert that the ethical thrust of the conciliar process is only bound up with the nature and function of the church (see no. 5). The document notes the assumption by the WCC that the idea of *koinonia* is the fundamental ecclesiological category. However, it asserts that the content of *koinonia* must be broadened by integrating the ethical dimension into it. The bond between faith and action, by virtue of which discipleship has given form to a style of community life and moral existence, is in fact a constant of Christian tradition. Even if it is not possible to assert that those who commit themselves to justice, peace and the preservation of creation *ipso facto* belong to the church, it is a constant fact of experience that a common commitment creates communities; it can therefore be said that an ecclesio-genetic force is at work in the communal battles undertaken in these spheres, one which often also illuminates doctrine. So *koinonia* in relation to the ethical does not primarily signify that the Christian community establishes rules and regulations, but rather that it is a place in which, though the confession of faith and the celebration of the sacraments, and as an inseparable part of it, the tradition of the churches is constantly examined. From it this tradition receives inspiration and intuition of a moral order. A constant ethical reference here keeps the themes of humankind and the world alive in the light of the gospel. In this way the community is also essentially a place of comfort and support. For some, this can amount to strong support for nonviolence; for others, it is a permanent response to the dimension of gift and forgiveness which is characteristic of the whole of human life; for yet others, it is an attempt to recover the sense of vocation and covenant in the experience of personal and social life. In every case, *koinonia* implies a proposal addressed to all human beings committed to a moral effort, who need structures and perspectives. In this way the moral life of the Christian community can be described as testimony, which is an essential aspect of it (see no. 19). Therefore the church itself can be defined as a moral community.

The particularity of ecclesial experience is here presented as action in service to the world, which promotes peace, justice and the preservation of creation. The problems which arise in this area have a twofold polarity, local and universal; they in fact always refer to concrete situations and at the same time have a global dimension. The action which they require is therefore always local and universal; it is commitment in the particular context which at the same time finds a place in the universal ecumene. The main problem raised by this vision of the unity of the church is the relation between ethical commitment in the world and church life centred on the faith and its sacraments.[9] This relation is not in fact clear, and the impression is not infrequently given that the intention to serve, as a corrective to a concept of church unity which forgets Christian responsibility in the world, tends imperceptibly to transform itself into an alternative definition of the church itself, in which faith and sacraments assume secondary importance. The church is certainly not an end in itself, but has to testify to the reconciliation which God offers to the world and make it historically perceptible. However, in some statements it seems that the reality of the church, with the elements which down history have characterized the understanding of its identity in a more pointed way, is mainly considered as a possible obstacle which risks blocking the movement that originates in God and is orientated on the world.[10]

Concluding observations

The examples given above were meant to suggest some of the orientations present in contemporary theological reflection on the unity of the church, though the panorama is more varied and complex, and the choices I have made might seem arbitrary to some. At the end of these reflections I would like to point to some open problems which theological reflection cannot ignore.

All the conceptions of church unity mentioned have a legitimacy deriving from the fact that they bring together aspects of the reality of the church. However, that necessarily involves a degree of partiality, above all where it is not simply a question of the most appropriate way to understand the church: there is a tendency to affirm exclusively an element which proves not to be sufficiently valued in other theological views. The way of dissolving ecclesiological theory, on the grounds that it is partial precisely because of its claim to universality, is not a true response to the problem. Rather, one can ask in what way ecclesiology can fulfil its task better, namely that of co-ordinating in a coherent overall view the components of church unity, also integrating dimensions which so far have been obscured.

A second feature common to many proposals is the emphasis on the need to bring out the particular character of church experience. That fits with the overcoming of an abstract view of unity which has led to an awareness of the importance of both church life and theological reflection. However, in some cases this leads to an absolutization of contextual particularity which in fact makes communication and reciprocal recognition impossible (e.g. because only those who have had a particular experience can understand and talk about it). An exclusive emphasis on particularity brings with it the risk of voiding of content discourse about the universal unity of believers in Christ. The cause of some of today's conflicts in the church can be seen precisely in the tendency to absolutize the particular. In extreme cases, such conflicts can in fact make the awareness of sharing one faith inoperable. The alternative way of making effective universal unity possible is to create a network of processes of communication which make possible not only awareness, understanding and reciprocal recognition but also criticism, among the experiences of the various churches. The institutional instruments created to guarantee universal unity can function only if they take up and sustain these processes of communication aimed at reciprocal recognition.

Finally, these processes of communication cannot have just any content, exclusively dictated by the needs of the present, with the consequence that a marginal role is attached to the faith which welcomes the Word of God and is expressed in the celebration of the sacraments. In the face of the tendency to relativize the profession of faith as a criterion of church unity over other elements, in this sphere too it seems to me important to emphasize the essentially visible character of the church. The mark of visibility says that the church exists only as a concrete subject in history. However, this requires that believers are capable of recognizing themselves as persons who profess the same faith; the awareness of belonging together is based on this foundation. So without forgetting the historicity of the doctrinal formulae and legitimate pluralism, ecclesial communion cannot dispense with consensus and a binding formulation of the common faith. In this question the problem of the development of a hermeneutic common to the Christian tradition arises. A Faith and Order study has been devoted to this topic which examines the process of discernment to be used in overcoming the confessional differences and giving expression to the one gospel in the different social and cultural contexts.

Translated by John Bowden

Notes

1. Cf. J. M. R. Tillard, *L'église locale. Ecclésiologie de communion et catholicité*, Paris 1995, 15–144.
2. See M. Kinnamon (ed.), *Signs of the Spirit. Official Report Seventh Assembly*, Geneva and Grand Rapids 1991, 173, for the official text.
3. Cf. O. Cullmann, *Einheit durch Vielfalt. Grundlegung und Beitrag zur Diskussion über die Möglichkeiten ihrer Verwicklung*, Tübingen 1986; id., *Les voies de l'unité chrétienne*, Paris 1992.
4. Cf. L. Klein, 'Theologische Alternative zur Konsensusökumene', *Theologische Quartalschrift* 166, 1986, 268–78.
5. Cf. H. Fries and K. Rahner, *Einigung der Kirche – reale Möglichkeit*, Quaestiones Disputatae 100, Freiburg im Breisgau 1983.
6. See ibid., 36.
7. Cf. K. Raiser, *Ökumene im Übergang. Paradigmenwechsel in der ökumenischen Bewegung?*, Munich 1989, 51–123.
8. Cf. T. Best and W. Granberg-Michaelson (eds), *Koinonia and Justice, Peace and Creation: Costly Unity. Presentations and Reports from the World Council of Churches' Consultation in Rønde, Denmark, February 1993*, Geneva 1993.
9. Because of the tendency to exclude this specifically ecclesial problem, H. Meyer argues that the conciliar process cannot be regarded as a model of church union in the real sense because it presupposes that communion of faith already exists between Christians and the churches; it therefore does not see it as a problem to be confronted and so does not perceive the need to relate it to the objective of the conciliar process (cf. H. Meyer, *Ökumenische Zielvorstellungen*, Göttingen 1996, 166–7). On the other hand, as Meyer himself recognizes, there is a problem in clarifying the relationship between the conciliar process and research carried on in other sections of the ecumenical movement with a theological definition of unity. It therefore seems that the unilateralism in the emphasis on the ethical element can represent, at least *de facto*, a real ecclesiological alternative.
10. For a broader analysis of the theological debate on unity see A. Maffeis, 'Modelli di unità della Chiesa nella storia del movemento ecumenico e nel dibattito teologico recente', *Teologia* 19, 1994, 62–93, 109–50.

II · The Past

Is the New Testament Canon the Basis for a Church in Fragments?

Hans Dieter Betz

The question whether the New Testament canon is the basis for a church in fragments[1] cannot be answered with a simple yes or no; because it has so many levels, it calls for a differentiated answer. Here I shall first of all discuss the state of affairs presupposed by the question and then offer an answer on the basis of historical research and the history of theology.

I. Towards understanding the question

The formulation of the topic combines both historical and theological pespectives; since they are not clearly such, first of all they need to be clarified.

1. As posed, the question presupposes agreement that there is one church and not many churches. It is further presupposed that this one church can exist in fact or as a possibility, either as a unity or in fragments. These fragments are the results of questionable developments which call for a foundation, whereas unity is given an almost metaphysical preference. According to this view, it is natural to see the churches as they really exist in history as being in fragments. By contrast, the one church is the subject of ecclesiology, according to which the church can exist legitimately only in its unity, whether as *ecclesia invisibilis* or as an eschatological hope for the future. Consequently it has to be said that 'fragment churches' cannot claim to understand themselves as 'churches' in the full sense, certainly not if they are united in the federation of a 'World Alliance of Churches'. From the perspective of church unity, the classification 'fragments' therefore *a priori* puts in question the self-understanding of those church associations which understand themselves as churches and not merely as fragments. Elsewhere, too, of course,

fragments are incomplete pieces of a lost whole which at best can be restored in an artificial way. But without at least an idea of the original whole, fragments are defective and inferior. They may be better than a total loss, but as such they can make no claim to full validity.

The formulation 'a church in fragments' can thus be understood in two ways. It can either mean that while there is only one church, this exists only in fragments. One could then put them together carefully like a broken jar and restore the original object. Or one can think of a mosaic which consists of small stones. An artist could compose quite different mosaics of these stones. Here all the stones are in principle of equal value, just as the mosaics which were composed of them could make a justified claim to equal artistic merit. Applied to the church, this would then mean that any particular case is one of many possibilities which has taken the form that we now know from the historical fragments. We have to accept it as it is, as 'a church in fragments'. In principle, in other circumstances it could have been different, but that is no objection to the fact that it has become what it now is. Thus it is of its nature to be fragmentary, but because it is so, it need not necessarily be either defective or inferior.

2. The phrase 'the basis for' can also be understood in different ways in connection with the New Testament canon. First, the expression could suggest that historically speaking it was the purpose and aim of the New Testament canon to provide the basis for a 'church in fragments'. This could be interpreted to mean either that the canon should make such a church possible and lead towards it, or that this should be legitimated after the event as already existing. The latter reading could then be extended to suggest that such a basis could also be useful in terms of the present church situation.

3. Since the question raised talks of the 'New Testament canon', it is appropriate to remind oneself of some basic facts.[2] Any view which thinks that it can ignore the Old Testament canon is problematical. For the fact is that the Christian canon of the Bible also had another unity in view, namely the coherence of the Old and New Testaments. This coherence was important in principle in that it established as dogma both the recognition of the Old Testament/Jewish origin of the church and canon and also the repudiation of the Marcionite canon with its rejection of the Old Testament and its restriction of the canon to a New Testament (heavily revised).[3] A church which wanted to base itself only on a New Testament canon would therefore *a priori* renounce a decisive aspect of church unity.[4]

Of course – and here is the justification for the limitation – then and now the New Testament canon is decisive for the foundation of what is to be understood by the church. But at the same time it has to be conceded that the early church took centuries to agree on a canon of the New Testament writings. So from a historical perspective the canon does not presuppose the church, but came into being contemporaneously with it. The canon is preceded by lists of the scriptures contained in it, all of which come from the second half of the first and the first third of the second century. However, even the New Testament writings did not precede the church, but attest its origin and development.

II. How was the New Testament canon formed?

The question of the origin of the New Testament canon raises an extraordinary complex problem, the details of which have formed a whole branch of research into the history of the canon.[5] The history of the New Testament canon embraces the history of the early church to the beginning of the Middle Ages. The canonization of the New Testament writings was the result of often tedious debates by church fathers and synods which need not be discussed here.

It is quite obvious that in principle the church fathers and synods which concerned themselves with the question of the canon had the unity of the church in view. But the creation of a binding canon of the Bible was only one of the means by which the unity of the church was to be safeguarded. The purpose of the canon was to select from the great wealth of Christian literature which was taking shape those writings which had authoritative and binding quality as documents of the initial apostolic age, which were used in the liturgical reading of scripture and preaching, and which were to be accepted and recognized as the foundation of church decisions. The selection was made from the perspective of the historical origin of the writings in question, depending on their already authoritative validity, their theological doctrine and their role in church politics *vis-à-vis* the so-called heretics. Here the aim of the canon was not only to safeguard the authoritative church tradition but also to exclude the extensive writings which ran contrary to the formation of the church tradition or seemed unsuitable as a basis for teaching.

It is important to be clear that the selection of writings was not made by modern historical-critical methods; that the verdicts on individual writings could change; and that controversies in church politics could have an influence. Nevertheless, in retrospect we can say that the representative writings which were most influential on the formation of church tradition and doctrine were contained in the New Testament canon from the beginning. The fact that by contrast the extensive writings of the so-called Apocrypha[6] and the Apostolic Fathers[7] were not accepted first meant that they were given no canonical status in respect of the formation of the church's doctrine. Another further consequence of canonization was that the dissemination of the writings of earliest Christianity concentrated on canonized Holy Scripture and that large parts of the non-canonical writings were neglected, forgotten, destroyed or declared heretical. The remnants of these writings which still exist today and which are only a fragment of those which once existed nevertheless prove to be very important for historical research into early Christianity. These writings are being slowly but steadily extended by rediscoveries, like those of the 'Teaching of the Twelve Apostles' (Didache)[8] or the Gnostic writings from Nag Hammadi,[9] and reconstructions of sources which were quoted in later writings and thus preserved.

The titles of the earliest Christian writings are the main element of the first lists of the canon.[10] These titles, some of which go back to later redaction of the writings concerned, were meant to bear witness to the origins of these writings in the initial apostolic age of the church. Other factors are not affected by canonization, like various manuscripts with divergent textual variants, original texts and languages, or theories about historical and theological origin, the incorporation of sources and redactional composition. The fact that the possibility of translating the texts was left open led to a flood of translations of the Bible in all languages of the world which continues to the present day.

Two conclusions, roughly speaking, can be drawn from the formation of the canon which has been sketched out in this way. First, the unity of the church was one of the declared goals by which the church fathers and synods allowed themselves to be influenced in their efforts to form the canon. Second, paradoxically the formation of the canon played an active part in the fragmentation of Christianity. The canonization of writings went hand in hand with the declaration that non-canonical writings were heretical and inferior and the suppression of them. The fact that different lists of the canon were linked with different kinds of churches in the East and West of the Roman empire also contributed to the fragmentation of Christianity. Although the differences in the lists of the canon are limited to a few writings which are not central, deeper-seated differences in tradition and doctrine underlie them. However, by and large it can be said today that despite all the differences and oppositions, Holy Scripture as a whole represents one of the strongest bonds in the efforts at church unity.

III. How did the writings of the New Testament come into being?

On the basis of the previous discussion it is evident that none of the writings brought together in the New Testament presupposes a New Testament canon at the time of its composition.

1. None of the New Testament writings is aware that one day it will

have canonical validity as Holy Scripture. Their ideas of the authority of scripture and doctrine are different. Even the notion of an Old Testament canon is not decisive in the New Testament. Certainly the Old Testament is cited and expounded as 'scripture', and mention is made of collections of groups of writings like 'Law and Prophets',[11] but as non-canonical texts can also be cited as 'scripture',[12] the boundaries of the Old Testament canon are not drawn sharply. The fact that the Old Testament is cited throughout from Greek translations means that the Septuagint is normative for the New Testament; however, the 'Septuagint canon' handed down by the Christian church has no canonical status in Judaism.[13]

2. The earliest writings of the New Testament are the writings of the apostle Paul. They were composed by him, sometimes with the help of collaborators, as authoritative documents; received by his communities, read aloud, handed down, and finally collected and edited. This was a complicated process which was only completed in the second century; its nature is only partly clear to us. The apostle's authority is in turn derived from the Lord of the church, Jesus Christ, who has commissioned him as an apostle, and from the will of God, by which the whole event of redemption is directed.[14]

However, there can be no question of a universal recognition of Paul's authority by the church during his lifetime or at a later date. As is evident from his letters and those of his disciples and followers, his figure, his theology and his influence in earliest Christianity were controversial. For his opponents, who are to be sought above all in rival Jewish Christianity, he was a heretic.[15] This controversial situation changed only when Jewish Christianity became a minority and collections of letters of Paul appeared around the middle of the second century. Certainly there are indications of a continuing Paul tradition, but its forms and extent are still largely obscure, as is the way in which the collection of letters which formed the presupposition for their inclusion in the canon was finally made.[16] It was one of the main services of Luke's Acts of the Apostles that it first worked out Paul's historical role for rising Christianity. The imitation of the Pauline letters by the so-called Deutero-Pauline letters (II Thessalonians, Colossians, Ephesians), and by I Clement and the letter of Ignatius, attests a development of literature which began early; however, no connection with the later collection of Paul's letters can be demonstrated. The historical effort represented by Luke's Acts of the Apostles also remained isolated and was not continued in the apocryphal Acts of Apostles in the second and third centuries.[17]

3. The four Gospels do not stand at the beginning but at the end of a lengthy process of tradition.[18] It took more than a generation after the death of Jesus before around 70 CE the author of the Gospel of Mark

presented an account of the life of Jesus. Here the decisive interest was in the Gentile Christian christology which had already been developed in the life of Jesus. However, that life first had to be reconstructed from earlier traditions. The author of the Gospel of Matthew, who was probably writing from another tradition around 90 CE, adapted the Gospel of Mark, heavily revising it and extending it. He had other traditions at his disposal, probably going back to Palestinian Jewish Christianity, above all the Matthaean Sermon on the Mount[19] and a version of the sayings source Q.[20] The Gospel of Matthew represents a new venture by comparison with Mark. The author of this 'book of the origin of Jesus Christ' (Matt. 1.1) wrote a life of Jesus in which Jesus and his teachings are derived historically and theologically from an Abrahamic Judaism (Matt. 1.1–12) in a way which at the same time also explains the origin of Christianity in the transition from Judaism to Gentile Christianity.[21] So this author did not limit himself to a life of Jesus, but at the same time narrated the basic features of a history of the church up to the return of Christ at the end of time. The author of the Gospel of Luke also used the Gospel of Mark, but he too revised it, since he was unsatisfied with his predecessors (Luke 1.1–4). He had another version of the sayings source Q and further special sources at his disposal. In contrast to Matthew, Luke wrote in two works a sketch of history which runs in a number of phases. The Gospel of Luke contains the life of Jesus as a prehistory of the time of the church, whereas the Acts of the Apostles makes the church begin with Jesus' ascension and the outpouring of the Holy Spirit at Pentecost and depicts its further extension up to the arrival of Paul in Rome. The Gospel of John takes yet another course. If it begins at all from the Gospel of Mark that we have and not from a further revision, it subjects all the traditions on which it draws to a theological critique, expands them, and enriches them by steeping them in a new spirit. This Gospel puts the emphasis on the theological transparency of the events and teachings in the life of Jesus.

To sum up, it may be said that the authors of the Gospels did not attribute any 'canonical' status to their sources as 'scripture' but very freely expressed the views of faith and historical notions contained in them in their own writings. While these writings treated the life of Jesus and the origin of the church in very different ways, their main interest lay in the unity of the church. We may further assume that the authors of the Gospels belonged to different trends in the church and that the traditions of these trends were handed down in their Gospels. However, that does not mean that the four Gospels are simply to be regarded as programmatic writings of such church trends, so that they bear witness to 'a church in four fragments'. Despite all the differences and oppositions which find expression in the four Gospels, each in its own way wanted to state the whole of the Gospel. Certainly they allow us to infer a literary rivalry between the authors, but these are not immediately to be identified with the groups which stand behind them, which fought against each other with the help of their Gospels.

IV. Do the writings of the New Testament bear witness to a church in fragments?

What do the New Testament writings say about the history of the origin of the church in a historical-critical perspective? At the beginning was there a church in fragments or a united church? Again, this is an extremely complicated question which does not allow of a simple answer. However, the New Testament sources give the historian sufficient material to form quite a detailed picture of Christianity as it developed.

We get a clear view of the beginnings, which are with Jesus and his disciples. As the Gospels show us, each in a different way, the disciples understood themselves by analogy with Judaism as pupils who gathered around their teacher and followed him. Thus they were neither a church nor a synagogue. However, already in the early I Thessalonians (2.14) and in Galatians (1.22), Paul mentions Christian communities in Judaea using the term 'churches' (*ekklesiai*). Whether these churches also used this term themselves, or whether Paul first attached it to them, cannot be decided. We do not have enough evidence. Once the term 'synagogue' (*synagoge*) is also applied to Christian communities.[22] In the Gospels the designation 'church' appears only twice in Matthew, who roots it historically as a promise of Jesus to Peter both in the life of Jesus (Matt. 16.18) and in church discipline (Matt. 18.17).

All the other passages in which 'church' (*ekklesia*) occurs relate to Diaspora communities in the mission area of Paul, who was also the first to introduce a theological concept of church. According to Paul, 'church' refers to all the local Christian communities,[23] which were founded in an orderly way by their apostle. These could exist as 'house communities' (*oikiai*),[24] which were held together by the overseer appointed for them (cf. Phil. 1.1) and shared worship. It is remarkable that Paul does not call the Christians in Rome to whom he wrote his letter to the Romans 'church', because he had not been active there in founding the church and only later as 'apostle to the Gentiles' (Rom. 11.13; 1.5) wanted to include the house churches there in his sphere of responsibility.[25]

If on first sight this picture looks like a 'church in fragments', we should note that according to Paul all these church communities were merely local branches of the one 'church of God'.[26] Initially Paul also agreed with the Jewish Christian authorities in Jerusalem that there can be only one church.[27] According to him, this one church is the body of the risen Jesus Christ who is present in it with his Spirit.[28]

Nevertheless this one church was not a sociologically simple entity from the beginning.[29] Certainly the church communities remained in touch with one another, above all through travelling delegations and letters, but there was no overarching organization. As Paul and Acts show, attempts were made in this direction from Jerusalem, but the missionary conference in Jerusalem already recognized that the rapid expansion of Gentile Christianity was beyond the capacity of the Jewish Christian authorities to control.

It was this conference which had to cope with the first fundamental crisis in the church.[30] All those who took part were agreed that legitimately there could be only one community of Christians. However, they were divided as to the way in which this could be achieved. According to Paul's account in Gal. 2.1–10 there was a trend which argued that all Gentile Christians should be circumcized as full proselytes and integrated into Judaism. The other option was a radical fragmentation into Jewish and Gentile Christianity. But the conference resolved on a third option, according to which it was recognized that the one God who is active not just within Judaism but throughout the world justifies two missionary strategies running in parallel. So agreement was reached on a formula according to which one mission operation, to the Jews, was to be led by the apostle Peter and the other, to non-Jews, was to be led by Paul (Gal. 2.8–9).

This solution was important for Paul, because he saw that a fragmentation of the church into Jewish and Gentile Christianity would theologically and in actual fact end up in polytheism. In contrast to polytheism, monotheism allowed only redemption by the one Christ and the one Spirit, and thus only a church made up of Jews and Gentiles.[31] In this church the link between Jews and Gentiles consists in the salvation-historical sequence 'first Jews, then Greeks',[32] and not therefore in separate ordinances of salvation for Jews and non-Jews. The traditional marks of distinction were felt to have been abolished within the one church as the 'new creation'.[33] Before the throne of God in the Last Judgment there is no respect of persons.[34] In the eschatological consummation of salvation, God will be all in all.[35]

However, the Jerusalem agreement soon shattered under the impact of historical events. In Antioch, when questioned by delegates from Jerusalem, Peter, Barnabas and other Jewish Christians withdrew from table fellowship with Gentile Christians under the leadership of Paul (Gal 2.11–14). According to Paul this step represented a denial of the unity of the church, whereas the Jewish Christians of Jerusalem perhaps insisted only that the arrangements made there should be kept. After that,

Jewish and Gentile Christians went their own ways, although attempts at mediation continued to be made. The conflict was provisionally brought to an end by the fact that following the Jewish wars against the Romans in 66–74 and 132–135 CE Jewish Christianity, too, was marginalized as a historically insignificant group.

But fragmentation also threatened rising Christianity at other points. As is evident from Paul's Corinthian correspondence, the disintegration of the community in Corinth as a result of party strife[36] and serious controversies with the apostle himself[37] could only be averted with extreme difficulty.[38] It emerges from the warnings against false teachers in a whole series of New Testament writings that conflicts over the right church teaching and practice arose at a very early stage not only in the Pauline communities but also elsewhere. Where orthodoxy took marked shape, almost of necessity those who thought otherwise came to be excluded, and they were then branded false teachers in propagandist terms. The fundamental conflict arose here primarily in sociological terms, as a result of ever greater variety, which began with the extension of Christianity, and through the orthodoxies which sought to impose unitary standards for church teaching and practice. Behind them stood theological efforts to guard against heresies by unification and preservation of Christian identity. Thus these conflicts themselves attest a theological awareness that despite all the multiplicity of Christianity in the end there can only be one church.

V. An attempt at a summary answer

So is the New Testament canon the basis for a church in fragments? After all that has been said, this question must be answered with a clear No. The church fathers and synods of the second to fourth centuries to whom we owe the formation of the canon had the unity of the church in mind when they brought together from a rapidly growing Christian literature those writings which documented the initial apostolic period and were to take on authoritative validity for the teaching and life of the church. The Holy Scripture which was authorized with this canon nevertheless comprised writings of heterogeneous origin which reflected a great variety of theological teachings, rites and forms of organization in the church. In the formation of the canon this multiplicity was not removed, say, by redactional censorship but left and thus confirmed, even where theological tensions and oppositions were visible. Thus for example the four Gospels were not fused into a Gospel harmony; the letter of James was set alongside the letters of Paul; although they came very close to heretical Gnosticism, the Johannine writings were accepted; and even the long-disputed Revelation of John was not refused entry into the canon.

This canon was created at a time in which the process of the expansion and differentiation of Christianity seemed to be beyond any institutional control and unification. Alongside the creeds, it was one of the theological and administrative means of restoring and preserving Christian identity in the varied form of church life with its many branches. It is inevitable that fragmentation should be introduced and encouraged where theological criteria are established and imposed. In this respect it will have to be said that historically the canon also contributed to a fragmentation of the church. On the other hand one must not expect too much of a canon. At no time was the canon of the Bible alone suitable for providing the basis of a church organization which spanned the world, for introducing it or for legitimating it.

Finally, in respect of today's church life it has to be said that the canon of Holy Scripture of the Old and New Testaments represents one of the few bonds of unity which comprises by far the greater part of otherwise diverging church organizations. The constant re-enactment of the central criteria established with Holy Scripture in worship, teaching and practice kept alive the awareness that the whole wealth of forms of church life finds fulfilment in the world before God not as a 'church in fragments', but in the admonitory words of the letter to the Ephesians (4.1–6):

> Lead a life worth of the calling to which you have been called, with all lowliness and meekness, with patience, forebearing one another in love, eager to maintain the unity of the spirit in the bond of peace. There is one body and one Spirit, just as you were called to the one hope that belongs to your call, one Lord, one faith, one baptism, one God and Father of us all, who is above all and through all and in all.

Translated by John Bowden

Notes

1. The question put to the author by the editors recalls the important lecture given by Ernst Käsemann in 1951, 'Is the New Testament Canon the Basis for the Unity of the Church?' (unfortunately the English translation of the lecture published in *Essays on New Testament Themes*, London 1964, 95–107, under the title 'The Canon on the New Testament and the Unity of the Church', obliterates the question form). See also the important articles in the article edited by Käsemann, *Das Neue Testament als Kanon. Dokumentation und kritische Analyse zur gegenwärtigen Diskussion*, Göttingen 1980. This article will not only consider these articles but also base itself on a wealth of investigations which have appeared in the meantime. They would really need every sentence to be annotated with footnotes, but this is impossible for reasons of space; consequently the notes must remain limited to some bibliographical indications of further reading.

2. The well-known book by Hans von Campenhausen, *The Formation of the Christian Bible*, London and Philadelphia 1972, is a good introduction.

3. For the terminology see Wilhelm Schneemelcher, in id. and R. McL. Wilson, *New Testament Apocrypha* (2 vols., Louisville and Cambridge 1991, 1992, I, 10–14.

4. For the problems see ibid., 15–33.

5. There are surveys of the history of the New Testament canon in W. G. Kümmel, *Introduction to the New Testament*, Nashville and London ²1975, 474–502; Wilhelm Schneemelcher, 'Bibel III. Die Entstehung des Kanons des Neuen Testaments und der Bibel,' *Theologische Realenzyklopädie* 6, 1980;, 22–48; Harry Y. Gamble, 'Canon: New Testament', *The Anchor Bible Dictionary* I, 1992, 852–61.

6. See Schneemelcher and Wilson, *New Testament Apocrypha* (n. 3).

7. See the edition of the Apostolic Fathers in the Loeb Classical Library ed. Kirsopp Lake, London 1912–13 (2 vols.); William R. Schoedel, 'Apostolic Fathers', *The Anchor Bible Dictionary* I, 1992, 313–16.

8. For the most recent state of scholarship see the commentary by Kurt Niederwimmer, *Die Didache*, Göttingen 1989.

9. There is a useful survey with bibliography in Birger A. Pearson, 'Nag Hammadi', *The Anchor Bible Dictionary* 4, 1992, 982–93. Cf. also the relevant section in Schneemelcher and Wilson, *New Testament Apocrypha* (n. 3); James M. Robinson, *The Nag Hammadi Library in English*, San Francisco ³1988; Kurt Rudolph, *Gnosis*, New York 1982.

10. See Schneemelcher and Wilson, *New Testament Apocrypha* (n. 3), I, 34–42.

11. Matt. 5.17; 7.12; 11.13; 22.40, etc. For a tripartite division cf. Luke 24.44: 'the writings in the Law of Moses, the Prophets and the Psalms'. See also my commentary *The Sermon on the Mount. A Commentary on the Sermon on the Mount, including the Sermon on the Plain (Matthew 5:3–7:27 and Luke 6:20–49)*, Hermeneia, Minneapolis 1995, 177–8.

12. Cf. Luke 11.49; John 7.38; I Cor. 2.9; James 4.5; Jude 14–15.

13. For this see Melvin K. H. Peters, 'Septuaginta', *The Anchor Bible Dictionary* 5, 1992, 1093–4, and Martin Hengel and Anna Maria Schwemer (eds.), *Die Septuaginta zwischen Judentum und Christentum*, Tübingen 1994.

14. Cf. the formulations in the prescripts to the letters: Rom. 1.1–7; I Cor. 1.1; II Cor. 1.1; Gal. 1.1 etc.

15. Cf. my article, 'Häresie. 1. Im Neuen Testament', *TRE* 14, 1985, 313–18; id., 'Heresy and Orthodoxy in the NT', *The Anchor Bible Dictionary* 3, 1992, 144–7.

16. Cf. Georg Strecker, *Literaturgeschichte des Neuen Testaments*, Göttingen 1992, 111–16.

17. Ibid., 243–57; cf. also Schneemelcher and Wilson, *New Testament Apocrypha* (n. 3), 80.

18. There is a survey in Strecker, *Literaturgeschichte* (n. 16), 122–3.

19. See my commentary mentioned in n. 11 above.

20. For the present state of research see the survey in Christopher M. Tuckett, 'Q (Gospel Source)', *The Anchor Bible Dictionary* 5, 1992, 567–72; Helmut Koester, *Ancient Christian Gospels. Their History and Development*, Philadelphia and London 1990, 49–171.

21. I have developed my views on the Gospel of Matthew further in 'The Sermon on the Mount in Matthew's Interpretation', in *Synoptische Studien, Gesammelte Aufsätze* II, Tübingen 1992, 270–89, esp. 286–7.

22. Cf. James 2.2; but also 5.14.

23. Cf. I Cor. 11.17–20, 33; 14.23, 26; Gal. 2.2.

24. Cf. I Cor. 1.16; 16.15,19; Rom. 16.5; Mark 10.29–30; Acts 11.14; 16.15, 31–32; 18.8; Col. 4.15; also Ernst Dassmann, 'Haus II (Hausgemeinschaft)', *Reallexikon für Antike und Christentum* 13, 1986, 886–94.

25. Cf. Rom. 1.5–7, 11–15; 15.22–24, 28–29.

26. For this term see I Thess. 1.1; 2.14; Gal. 1.13; I Cor. 1.2; 4.17; 10.32; 11.16,22; 12.28.

27. Cf. Gal. 2.1–10; Rom. 15.25–29.

28. For the doctrine of the church as the body of Christ see Gal. 3.26–28; I Cor. 6.15; 10.16–17; 11.27,29; 12.4–30; Rom. 3.8.

29. For what follows see my 'Paul', *The Anchor Bible Dictionary* 5, 1992, 186–201; id., *Paulinische Studien, Gesammelte Aufsätze* III, Tübingen 1994.

30. For what follows see my *Galatians. A Commentary on Paul's Letter to the Churches in Galatia*, Hermeneia, Philadelphia 1979, 81–103.

31. Cf. I Cor. 8.5–6; I Thess. 1.9–10; Gal. 3.26–28; I Cor. 12.13; Rom. 1.14; 10.12.

32. Cf. Rom. 1.16; 2.9–10; 15.27; I Cor. 1.22–23.

33. Cf. Gal. 3.28; 5.6; 6.15; I Cor. 7.19; Rom. 2.25–29.

34. Cf. II Cor. 5.10; Rom. 2.11; 14.10–12.

35. Cf. I Cor. 15.23–28; Rom. 11.30–32.

36. See above all I Cor. 1.10–17; 3.3–9 and the investigation by Margaret M. Mitchell, *Paul and the Rhetoric of Reconciliation. An Exegetical Investigation of the Language and Composition of I Corinthians*, Tübingen 1991.

37. See above all II Cor. 10.1–13.10 and my *Die Apostel Paulus und die sokratische Tradition. Eine exegetische Untersuchung zu seiner 'Apologie' 2 Korinther* 10–13, Tübingen 1972.

38. For an account of events and a sketch of the history of research see my *2 Corinthians 8 and 9. A Commentary on Two Administrative Letters of the Apostle Paul*, Hermeneia, Philadelphia 1985.

A Lost Fragment: Jewish Christianity

Ulrich H. J. Körtner

I. The churches and Judaism

The beginnings of Christianity lie in Judaism. That is by no means just a succinct historical statement, but a fact of enormous significance for systematic theology. The relationship of the Christian churches to Judaism and the overcoming of centuries of Christian hostility to the Jews is the decisive problem of ecumenical theology and thus also of any ecclesiology. Thus the attitude of the churches to Judaism in history and the present must also be understood as a central topic of the study of the confessions or of ecumenical Christianity. In my view it is a serious defect, not only of earlier accounts of these questions but also of more recent accounts of a study of the churches which sees itself as being explicitly ecumenical, that this topic is either totally neglected or its special features are passed over in favour of an ecumene of all religions.[1]

A systematic ecclesiology and a descriptive study of the churches which take account of the abiding existence of Judaism make it necessary to redefine the ecumenical concept of unity in quite a new way. Ecclesiological thought then has to be shifted from the concept of unity to that of difference. The issue is the paradoxical unity of difference in identity and difference in Christianity which in turn is to be defined in relation to Judaism. The differentiation in the unity of Christianity includes not only the distinction between belief in one church and its particular denominational forms, but also that between the church and the people of God on the one hand, and on the other the distinction between the people of God as an eschatological entity and empirical Judaism or Israel. The fundamental problem of ecumenism is not the unity of the church but the unity of the people of God, whose exclusive identity with the church could only be asserted as long as Judaism was declared a thing of the past by Christianity.

In so far as merely the visible unity of the churches is formulated as a goal by the ecumenical movement, ecumenical theology falls short of the eschatological and ecclesiological perspectives of the New Testament. Conversely, an ecumenical theology which incorporates the relationship of the churches to Judaism into its ecclesiological reflection will set far more modest limits to the aims of the ecumenical movement than usually happens. An ecumenical theology orientated on the concept of difference leads to the concept of a theory of the people of God in fragments. The concept of the fragment points to the ambiguity of all historical and social phenomena, as it expresses both the legitimate plurality of the fellowship brought about by the Spirit and also sinful divisions, alienation and conflict. Finally, it also expresses the eschatological perspective of an ultimate consummation of all life which we human beings cannot achieve by ourselves.

The paradoxical unity of identity and difference in Christianity is concentrated in Jewish Christianity.[2] This, too, is by no means just a phenomenon of the past, but also exists today in very different species.[3] So the phenomenon of Jewish Christianity or a contemporary messianic Judaism shows that not only the historical origin but also the present existence of Christianity is inseparably bound up with Judaism. As a link between synagogue and church, Jewish Christianity bears witness in history and the present over against the synagogue that the will of God revealed in the Old Testament and his promises are finally disclosed and realized through the Christ event. Over against the church, it not only emphasizes the Jewish legacy, but in addition represents the abiding claim of Israel to be the people of the divine promise. On the other hand, Jewish Christianity in particular embodies the paradox of belief in the unity of the people of God made up of Jews and Gentiles, in so far as baptized Jews often become aliens in the church and at the same time are cast out by their own people.

But Jewish Christianity in particular also embodies the conflict which runs through history between orthodoxy and heresy, and challenges an ecumenical theology to think through these categories critically. Wide stretches of the history of Jewish Christianity testify to the way in which it was branded heretical by the mainstream Gentile Christian church which came to be established, and which aimed at a strict demarcation from Judaism. In respect of Judaism it is therefore important to subject the anti-Jewish implications of the traditional church concept of heresy to a theological critique.

II. The concept of Jewish Christianity

However, the term 'Jewish Christians' is ambiguous, whether the context is the history of religion or the study of confessions. First, a distinction can be made between a historical-genetic and an ideological definition.

According to the former, all Christians who were born Jews are part of Jewish Christianity. According to the latter, any content of Christian teaching which can be derived from Judaism is to be defined as Jewish Christian. But such a broad concept is hardly suitable for gaining a precise grasp of Jewish Christianity as a historical phenomenon or as a contemporary phenomenon. It is therefore worth having a narrower, genetic concept of Jewish Christianity.

Yet again, a genetic concept of Christianity is ambiguous, in that in late antiquity a distinction needs to be made between Palestinian and Diaspora Judaism; between Pharisaic, Sadducean or Essene Judaism; or between Galilean and Alexandrian Judaism. And even contemporary Judaism does not represent a homogeneous entity, but can be differentiated into Sephardic and Ashkenasy Judaism; Orthodox, Conservative, Reform or Liberal Judaism; Judaism in Israel and Judaism in the Diaspora; to mention only the most important distinctions.

In history and the present, Jewish Christianity has applied to itself or has had applied to it by others a whole series of designations. The term 'Ebionite' to describe it is particularly widespread in the literature of the early church. This is derived from the Hebrew *'ebyonim* ('poor'), with which a Jewish Christian group described itself as being poor before God, i.e. as pious. Origen used this self-designation ironically to indicate the supposed dearth of theological capacity among Jewish Christians, and with such negative associations the term 'Ebionites' became a designation of Jewish Christianity generally in the heresiologies of the third and fourth century. A further name of Jewish Christians was 'Nazarenes', which according to Epiphanius is derived from Nazareth as Jesus' place of origin, but has nothing to do with the pre-Christian sect of the Nasoreans. Occasionally the term 'Hebrews' is also applied to the Jewish Christians in late antiquity. Jewish Christian groups known from the patristic literature include the Elkesaites and the Symmachians.

Modern Jewish Christianity similarly comprises very different groups. To distinguish them from the Jewish Christians of the first century an attempt has been made to find new designations. Thus people talk either of Messianic Jews or of Hebrew Christians. Jews who believe in Christ can, however, be found within churches stamped by Gentile Christianity and outside these in independent groups. So today the concept of Jewish Christianity is also by no means clear.

III. The history and theology of historical Jewish Christianity

Historical Jewish Christianity had a much greater geographical extension and theological variety than seems to be the case in the polemical accounts of the heresiologists of the early church. The earliest sources for Jewish Christianity are the writings of the New Testament and the Christian writings from the New Testament period which were not canonized. Towering figures of early Jewish Christianity include the apostle Peter and James the brother of the Lord. Peter, who as one of the first witnesses to the resurrection of Jesus was an outstanding figure of the Jerusalem community, went beyond the frontiers of Palestine and engaged in mission among the Jews in the Diaspora. Evidently Peter was the representative of a mild Jewish Christianity which asserted that the Torah continued to be law for baptized Jews, but granted the legitimacy of a mission to the Gentiles free of the law of the kind being practised by Paul, who was born a Diaspora Jew. However, under James the brother of the Lord, who replaced Peter as leader of the community, the Christian community in Jerusalem increasingly distanced itself from Peter's relatively liberal attitude and also attempted to make pagans who had become Christians observe the Torah. Still, James was evidently not among the rigorous 'Judaizers' who were vigorously contested by Paul, but one of the Jewish Christians who observed the law strictly and called for a symbiosis between Jewish Christianity and the Jewish people. Scholars argue over the position of the so-called Stephen circle in Jerusalem (cf. Acts 6.1ff.). Presumably the so-called Hellenists and Hebrews in the earliest Jerusalem community were not divided theologically, but merely linguistically.

The relationship between Paul and both Judaism and Jewish Christianity represents a special problem. Paul had to engage in controversy, not least with the representatives of Palestinian Jewish Christianity. Paul accepts the fact that Jews who have been baptized follow a Jewish lifestyle and observe the Torah, but strictly rejects the extension of this observance, even including circumcision, to non-Jews on the basis of his doctrine of justification and his understanding of the Torah. Paul's attitude to Judaism, which disputes the messiahship of Jesus, is also a complex one. On the one hand, according to Paul the church is in an irresolvable theological conflict with Judaism, which is why in Rom. 9.11 the apostle postpones the salvation of the Jewish people into the future. On the other hand, he believes that the promises of God to his people Israel continue to be valid, so that the Gentile church has to remain in contact with its Jewish roots.

The pre-synoptic sayings collection Q is also concerned to preserve the link between church and synagogue. At the latest, however, the Gospel of John reflects the increasing separation of church and synagogue, on the basis of the experience of the exclusion of Christians from the synagogue. However, the extent to which a Jewish Christian community stands behind the Gospel of John itself is a matter of dispute among scholars.

However much the first Christians who came from Judaism were concerned to maintain contact with their Jewish people and its religion, the christological confession which separated them from Judaism determined the self-understanding of their communities. The Jewish notion of election was transferred to the eschatological community of those who believed in Christ, and knew themselves to be in possession of the divine spirit which was bestowed on believers through baptism. But it is extremely difficult to reconstruct the theology or the community understanding of the first Jewish Christians in detail and to determine their relationship to the person and the religion of Jesus.

It has to be maintained that the first Christians understood themselves as part of Judaism. It was only the extension of the Christian mission beyond the frontiers of Palestine and the Jewish Diaspora communities, as a result of which the Gentile Christian church increasingly became an independent entity, and the parallel process of rejection by the synagogue, that led to an increase in the distance between Christianity and Judaism. However, in no way may the end of the earliest Jerusalem community be identified with the end of historical Jewish Christianity after the Bar Kochba revolt in 135 CE. Rather, from the time of Peter's mission to the Jews, in many parts of the Roman empire Jewish Christian communities had come into being which attempted to preserve the Jewish heritage and to emphasize the abiding significance of the Torah even for Gentile Christians. Alongside the Jewish Christian remnants in Transjordan (Pella), this applies above all to Syria and Asia Minor in the second century.

Towards the end of the second century, though, a move by the Gentile Christian church to declare Jewish Christianity heretical set in from the West. Mention should be made above all of the heresiologies of Irenaeus of Lyons and Hippolytus of Rome. Thus the Jewish Christians were said above all to have a heretical, 'natural' christology as they disputed the virgin birth of Jesus. In the East, however, in the third century the picture of Jewish Christianity is still much more complex, not least because Origen, Eusebius of Caesarea and even Jerome had a personal knowledge of Jewish Christianity. Jerome, who spent long years in Palestine, states the problems of the Jewish Christians very pointedly: 'As they want to be Jews and Christians, they are neither Jews nor Christians' (*Ep.* 112.13).

Numerous texts from the early church show that Jewish Christianity also remained an important factor in the period when the Gentile Christian mainstream church was becoming established. Its influence can be demonstrated in writings like the *Didascalia Apostolorum* (first half of the third century); the Pseudo-Clementines, a series of writings pseudonymously attributed to Peter; and in some texts of the Nag Hammadi Codices, though not all these are to be claimed for Jewish Christianity: they belong to the complex spectrum of Gnosticism. Jewish Christian influences can be demonstrated in Mandaeanism, Manichaeism and finally even in Islam.

IV. Messianic Judaism

After the downfall of the Jewish Christianity of the early church there can no longer be said to have been a homogenous Jewish Christianity. But in modern times a new form of Jewish Christianity has arisen alongside the churches stamped by Gentile Christianity. In the seventeenth century, a feeling of alienation in the church led baptized Jews to hold first meetings. In the second half of the nineteenth century first Jewish Christian communities came into being in Eastern Jewry, which remained largely untouched by the post-Enlightenment Jewish emancipation. Jechiel Lichtenstein (1831–1921), Joesef Rabinowitsch (1837–1899) and Theophil Lucky (1854–1916) were important representatives of Eastern European Jewish Christianity. In 1813 the association of the 'Sons of Abraham' was founded in London; in some respects it can be seen as a forerunner of the 'Jewish Christian Alliance' which formed in 1865. The International Hebrew Christian Alliance (IHCA) was founded in 1925.

It is estimated that today there are between 50,000 and 100,000 Jewish Christians, most of whom live in the USA. But there are also Jewish Christian groups, or groups which believe in the Messiah, in Israel. The situation of Jewish Christians in the present-day state of Israel reflects the complex conditions of the Diaspora. So a distinction needs to be made between those Jewish Christians who have found their religious home in one of the historical churches and those who have formed more or less special Jewish Christian groups.

The theological differences are considerable, particularly in understandings of the church. The relationship between messianic Jewish communities and the historical churches, the majority of whose members are Arab, is also complicated. Often some communities hardly know of the existence of others. As the Jewish-Christian movement in Israel avoids publicity, very little is known about it. The number of messianic Jews in Israel is estimated at 3,000. Their number is slowly growing as a result of the immigration of Jewish Christians from the USA. However, they cannot immigrate into Israel legally under the 'law of return'. The incomprehension that they meet with in Israel and the aversion to any form of mission there makes the situation of the messianic Jews extremely difficult.

As I remarked at the beginning, Judaism embodies in a unique way the paradoxical unity of identity and difference in Christianity, the tense juxtaposition of church and Judaism; people of God, church and Israel.

Menachem Ben Hayim, the secretary of the IHCA in Israel, has described this difficult position of Jewish Christianity as follows: 'We share in the offence caused by Gentile Christianity; and what seems even more absurd, we do not cease to hope for an even greater offence caused by Jewish Christianity.'[4] That applies equally both towards Judaism and towards Gentile Christianity. Like the historic Jewish Christianity of the first centuries, messianic Judaism in our day represents the people of Israel within the church. So it not only remembers the promises addresssed to Israel, but can also help to counter the tendency of churches stamped by the Gentile Christian tradition towards docetism and a spiritualizing of Christianity. But above all it is a challenge to examine critically the models for unity so far put forward by the ecumenical movement and to develop an ecclesiology in Jewish-Christian dialogue.

A certain tragedy for Jewish Christianity has always lain in the paradox of ecumenical unity in the field of tension between church and synagogue. Whereas in its first centuries Jewish Christianity fell victim to the need to separate Christianity from Judaism, today it threatens to suffer the fate of a lost fragment, because it now seems to stand in the way of the general need for the renewal of the relationship between church and synagogue and efforts towards a real Christian-Jewish dialogue. As for the development in Israel, it is at any rate an open question whether the second generation of messianic Jews continues to identify with this movement or, in so far as it is not taken up into the various traditional churches, it returns to Judaism. Thus present-day Jewish Christianity is an endangered fragment. One hopes that it does not get lost.

Translated by John Bowden

Notes

1. Cf. U. Körtner, 'Volk Gottes – Kirche – Israel. Das Verhältnis der Kirchen zum Judentum als Thema ökumenischer Kirchenkunde und ökumenischer Theologie', *ZKT* 91, 1993, 51–57.

2. For the history of Jewish Christianity see G. Strecker, 'Judenchristentum', *TRE* 17, Berlin and New York 1988, 318–25; W. G. Kümmel and F. Majer-Leonhard, 'Judenchristentum', *RGG³* III, Tübingen 1959, 967–72; H.-J. Schoeps, *Theologie und Geschichte des Judenchristentums*, Tübingen 1949; J. Daniélou, *Théologie du Judéo-Christianisme*, Tournai 1958; F. Manns, *Bibliographie du Judéo-Christianisme*, SBFA 13, Jerusalem 1979; W. Bauer, *Orthodoxy and Heresy in Earliest Christianity*, Philadelphia and London 1967; A. F. J. Klijn and G. J. Reinink, *Patristic Evidence for Jewish-Christian Sects*, NT.S 36, Leiden 1973; B. Bagatti, *The Church from the Circumcision. History and Archaeology of the Judaeo-Christians*, Jerusalem 1971.

3. For modern Jewish Christianity see K. Kjaer-Hansen and O. C. M. Kvarme, *Messianische Juden. Judenchristen in Israel*, Erlangen 1983; S. Schoon, *Christliche Präsenz im judischen Staat*, Berlin 1986; H. D. Leuner, *Zwischen Israel und den Völkern. Vorträge eines Judenchristen*, Berlin 1978; A. G. Fruchtenbaum, *Hebrew Christianity. Its Theology, History and Philosophy*, Grand Rapids 1974; M. Schiffmann, *Return of the Remnant. The Rebirth of Messianic Judaism*, Baltimore 1992; D. Stern, *Messianic Jewish Manifesto*, Jerusalem 1988.

4. M. B. Hayim, 'Jesus facing the Messianic Jew Today', in O. C. Kvarme (ed.), *Let Jews and Arabs Hear His Voice*, Jerusalem 1981, 14.

In the Footsteps of the Apostolic Churches: Fragmentation and Unity in the Christian West

Lorenzo Perrone

A neglected historical horizon

A frequent mistake made from the perspective of Western Christianity in considering the problem of the fragmentation of the church is that this perspective tends to associate the fragmentation essentially with two episodes: the schism between the Latins and Greeks conventionally dated to 1054, and subsequently the separation in Western Christianity of the churches arising out of the Reformation. This simplification ignores the fact that there had already been deep fractures in the body of the church. Thus it is worth adding straight away that the idea of a 'united' church belongs in the role of myth. It does not make sense to shift confirmation of the first breaks in the church backwards, from the eleventh century to the fifth, since the dialectic between unity and separation can be seen from the first centuries on. This fact is amply confirmed in historical studies of primitive Christianity, though it can be seen positively as 'pluralism'. The term 'pluralism' denotes a fertile wealth of differing phenomena, but when these become exclusive or conflicting, they contain within themselves the germs of separation. To some degree we can read the history of the church in the first centuries as a continuous effort to compromise between its pluralism and the demands of unity. The historical phases, first of so-called 'proto-catholicism' and then of the 'imperial church', are both responses, albeit in different forms, to the need for unity at the level of both discipline and doctrine, especially at this second level. However, like other breaks which emerged before or after them, the rents in Eastern Christianity preceding or following the Council of Chalcedon (451), in the framework of the great christological controversies of the fifth and sixth centuries, bear witness to the value of the fragment or, better, show that unity cannot be had at any price.

This ancient episode of fragmentation is all the more significant if one remembers its historical and geographical scope: it came about in the churches which are the direct continuation of the apostolic communities, on territory which was originally influenced by these churches or their dependents, from Syria to Egypt. Moreover, there was a dynamic of growing expansion over the centuries, from Armenia to Ethiopia, and from Mesopotamia to China and India. Up to the beginning of the modern era this complex of churches – which today we prefer to call 'Eastern Orthodox Churches', abandoning the traditional polemical labels 'Nestorian' and 'Monophysite' – represented the most conspicuous missionary expansion of Christianity, above all thanks to the extraordinary penetration of the Syrian Eastern Church in Asia. The sometimes litigious particularism of their 'rites' has all too easily caused the historical merits of these churches to be forgotten. Above all in modern times, this factor has disconcerted more than one observer, and has led to this phenomenon being judged a largely superstitious survival, contrasting not only with Christian universalism but also with the 'superior' religion of Islam.[1]

Dynamics of fragmentation: doctrinal reasons and political, ethnic and cultural particularisms

In any case, fragmentation is not an easy process, to be welcomed with a light heart, even if one has the conviction of possessing the truth, as was the case with the 'Monophysites' who opposed the 'Chalcedonian' Byzantine church. The 'Nestorian' Christians of Persia, hampered by the political domination of the Sassanids, the rivals of Byzantium for the control of the Middle East, are a different story. This political encumbrance was the reason why at the end of the fifth century they claimed autocephaly (424) and doctrinal independence (484) from the imperial church. And for the 'Monophysites' of Syria and Egypt, a full and irreparable separation took place only after a notable lapse of time, towards the middle of the sixth century. Does this show a concern to remain united in the same church, despite the vexations suffered in the name of political and dogmatic uniformity, the determining factor leading to isolation as a fragment of a church which was formerly one?

An adequate answer would have to recognize the multiplicity of the factors which combine to lead to ecclesial fragmentation as they relate to the specific features of the individual areas of the East where fragmentation took place. All in all, it would seem right to recall that the doctrinal motives, serious and real as they appeared at the time (rather than being mainly terminological, as they tend to appear now, at a distance, in present-day ecumenical dialogue), did not play an exclusive role. They were associated with other causes, sometimes of equal weight. Thus dogmatic differentiation from the imperial church satisfied some needs for political, ethnic or national, linguistic and cultural autonomy, as happened with the emergence of the 'national' Armenian, Coptic and Ethiopian churches or with the self-assertion of the Western Syrian Church, which had been able to graft indigenous Semitic traditions on to the common stem of Hellenization.[2] All in all, resistance to homo-logization played an important role, although a full evaluation of the recovery of local autonomy at the ecclesial level would have to include an examination of doctrinal contrasts. Schematically these can be re-duced to the current theological alternatives of Alexandria and Antioch, the two key elements in which were biblical interpretation and the christological reflection of the Greek fathers. Alexandria, intent above all on allegorical exegesis and the initiative of the Logos in the incarna-tion, has remained the point of reference for the family of 'Monophysite' churches; Antioch, preoccupied with safeguarding the man in the in-carnate Logos, and also with a preference for literal exegesis, provided the anchorage for the 'Nestorian' churches. However, the processes of confessionalization go beyond the antagonism between the two 'schools' and their respective christological models, and are to be connected not only with a desire to withdraw from the suffocating embrace of the Byzantine church and empire but also with the changes in historical context which arose with the advent of Islamic domination. The new masters favoured the formation of true religious 'ethnic' groupings in accordance with an institutional legal formula (best exemplified by the Ottoman system of the *millet* or 'nation') which was to remain substanti-ally in force down to the threshold of our era.[3] The internal cohesion of the individual communities then became a condition for their very survival in the limited areas of life allowed by the Islamic power, imposing a regime of vigilant defence of the group's 'rite' – *the* dis-tinctive feature among the various forms taken by the life of the community, and as such a crystallizing element of religious identity. Finally, simplifying the somewhat complex dynamic of ecclesial fragmentation to the utmost, one can see how in the Christian East a doctrinal diversity which was certainly not secondary on the one hand encouraged churches to affirm themselves on political, ethnic and cul-tural bases distinct from the Byzantine ambience, and on the other allowed the diversities thus acquired to be safeguarded within a new regime, extraneous to the Christian religion. However, in the long term this was not without grave costs to the spiritual and cultural vitality of these communities.

Beyond the particularisms: the dimensions of church unity

The multiform image of the ethnic and religious particularisms of the Christian East must not mislead us: the multiple church fragmentation reflects a series of shared dimensions, more than appears on a superficial examination. These churches in fact prove to belong to a common tradition and historical experience – of which they were more or less aware – which is broader than their individual expressions. Beyond all the reasons for fragmentation indicated above, note has to be taken in the first place of the common bond of faith in Christ, experienced with emphases which remain typical of Orthodox Christianity, to the detriment of the primitive detachment from this. These include the preference for a *theologia gloriae* in the vision of the Christian mystery, an attachment to the biblical and patristic tradition, a mystical and eschatological calling rather than a practical or a theoretical one, accompanied by the centrality of monastic experience as a form of Christian life. Furthermore, the basic continuity with the Byzantine church has also been recognized in ecclesiology, the sacraments, the cult of the Virgin and the saints.[4] Several essential premises contributed towards assuring these convergences in the formative phrase: thus, the common Hellenistic foundations which lie at the beginnings of the propagation of Christianity in this vast geographical area continued to operate subsequently. Combined with the local languages and cultures, as we have seen, they became an element in their emancipation. It is no accident that these churches, leaving confessional oppositions aside, played an active part in mediating classical culture (philosophical, scientific and legal) to the Arab world, as happened particularly in Syria and Mesopotamia, both with the Jacobite 'Monophysite' church and the Persian 'Nestorian' church. Moreover, from antiquity to the late Middle Ages they engaged in important processes of religious and cultural interaction which led to a wide circulation of forms of spirituality and hagiographical traditions.[5] The interchanges were helped by situations which can be defined within certain limits as 'ecumenical', at least in the sense that they arose from relations in which the various churches existed together in a secular world. Thus it was natural that a centre like Jerusalem, which traditionally has had the greatest concentration of different Christian communities, assumed a decisive function in this respect, thus continuing the original apostolic mission.[6]

On the other hand, there have been efforts to justify the reality of ecclesial fragmentation from a theological perspective; these seek to reshape or transcend the aspect of separation. Generally speaking, we can reduce the various formulas to a common call for fidelity to apostolic origins. They draw, for example, on foundation legends, like the preaching of the apostle Bartholomew in the case of the Armenian tradition, or the recollection of the eunuch converted by Philip (Acts 8.27–39), who is appealed to as founder of the Christian tradition of Ethiopia. Without any legendary elaboration, there is an appeal to continuity with the apostolic faith as a pledge of orthodoxy and fidelity to the tradition of the fathers. For Abdisho (or Ebedjesus), Metropolitan of Nisibis (died 1318), this link guarantees the authentic character of the Eastern Syrian Church, and its universal status as a true representative of the *catholica*. In such claims, pride of place goes to the notion of a sequence of 'fathers' which cannot be reduced simply to invoking the theological authorities peculiar to the two distinct dogmatic traditions (Cyril of Alexandria for the 'Monophysite' churches and Theodore of Mopsuestia for the 'Nestorian' churches respectively). The testimony of the councils of the early church is an indispensable part of the patristic heritage, and particularly the Niceno-Constantinopolitan Creed, which is accepted by all as a manifestation of the common faith. As is very clear in the profession of faith by the Persian Synod of Mar Sabrisho (596), the awareness of following in the footsteps of the fathers makes it possible to get beyond the horizon of fragmentation and link up with a wider communion of the faithful: the faith of the fathers and the Orthodox faith, which is shared by all right-minded believers.[7] Even where the ecclesial perspective might seem mainly conditioned by the encumbrance of nationalism – as, at first sight, is the situation of the Armenian church – the link with the confession of the fathers firmly binds the ecclesial community to its apostolic and patristic roots, as a greatness which transcends the narrow confines of the nation-church.

Another way is often taken to justify the existence of separate churches, not only from the aspect of faith, but with the aim of arriving at a legitimization on the legal and institutional level. This is an emphasis on the reality of the local church, given a distinct form by geographical, political and national factors. Thus the Eastern Syrian Church significantly gives itself the title 'church of the East', which brings out the merit of its autocephaly as a territorial, particular and autonomous articulation of the one body of the church. This type of justification, too, goes back to the ecclesiology of apostolic times and the patristic tradition, for which the dimension of the local church gives expression to the communion of the universal church.[8] Nor can the establishment of 'five patriarchates' (pentarchy) in connection with the explosion of christo-logical conflicts in the fifth century be seen as a contradiction to this, since it, too, hinges on the notion of distinct regional ambits, albeit gathered around a mother church of apostolic origin (or claiming to be of apostolic origin).[9] The synodal seal which brings distinctions within the Eastern churches, and which comes to give considerable room for the participation of the laity in the life of the church, also belongs on the same line.[10]

To these various modes of perceiving and putting into practice the dimensions of church unity within the particularism of the Christian East must be added another, the decisive significance of which is manifested today in an even more notable form that is shared almost by all: the awareness that there is no longer any reason for the splits between the confessions. Now that the most bitter phase of polemic and reciprocal excommunications is over, there has been an acceptance – albeit only occasional and demonstrated by some particular figures – of the substantial doctrinal convergence in the face of the 'nominalism' which is said to have marked the disputes of the past. Little by little it is being noted that the dogmatic oppositions over the union of the divine and human natures in Christ in reality reflect the same content of faith in different formulations.[11] The adoption of these positions was facilitated by the inter-religious confrontation with Islam, which promoted the Christians of the various confessions to adopt a more unified position. However, it is rarely that we find professions of real ecumenism *avant la lettre*, like that of the great Armenian Catholicos Nerses Shnorhali in the twelfth century. In his readiness for union with the Byzantine church he was moved by the conviction, among other things, of the conventional nature and relativity of theological language, which made it impossible to impose a formulation as exclusive.[12]

Moreover, the impulses towards church reunification had to revolve around the issues of the moment. Once the Islamic control slackened, the Eastern churches were brought into a more direct confrontation with the rest of Christianity. This happened especially through the unionist policy developed by the Roman see on the wave of the First Crusade and subsequently with many attempts which had different outcomes, down to modern times. Looked at in the historical and theological context, these forces could not fail to attract a somewhat negative verdict, though with some important distinctions, since the model which they followed was rooted to a large degree in the absorption of these communities into Roman Catholicism with the consequent Latinization. With good reason, the unionist policy caused conflicts within the individual communities leading to a further fragmentation in the front presented by the Eastern churches, which was already a composite one.[13]

That contributed towards weakening the complex force of Christian testimony, which for centuries had been directed at the challenge with

Islam in a regime almost always characterized by conditions which were unfavourable, if not directly hostile, to Christianity. But this same historical situation makes the Eastern churches a particularly interesting observatory for a 'post-Christian' situation. At the same time, the terms of religious confrontation, at least for some of these communities, were further broadened by competition from other 'world religions' of antiquity, far beyond the 'peoples of the Book', which were more familiar to the Christians of the Greek and Latin world up to the advent of the modern era. Thus the Eastern Syrian Church, through its own missionary dynamic, had to compete with Manichaeanism, Buddhism, Confucianism and Taoism, offering models of 'inculturation' of the Christian faith – from relations with the Chinese religious context to the Shamanism of Central Asia – which anticipated the complex difficulties of evangelization today.[14]

From the past to the future: openings towards a reshaping of the church

The Christian substance of this past of the 'Eastern Orthodox Churches' has emerged in a new light through the ecumenical dialogues of the last three decades. These dialogues have restored vigour to the prophetic intuitions of some of their precursors, by developing awareness of both of the strength and the particular limits of the individual fragments of the church which emerged in the shadow of opposed doctrinal traditions. Here not only the negative experience of fracture has been noted but also its positive aspects, as a partial and legitimate expression of the wider and inexhaustible 'mystery' of Christ over which the manifestation of which other expressions, also legitimate but limited, compete.

This is the most significant result so far arrived at by the new season of encounters with the Christian East, which has found its manifesto and dynamic point of reference in the 1971 'Christological Declaration of Vienna'. After taking up the traces of the peace agreement between Alexandria and Antioch which followed the Council of Ephesus in 433, this declaration affirms that the human spirit will never be in a position to understand and express fully the mystery of Christ, and expresses confidence that the various ecclesial and theological traditions will be able to reshape themselves in the light of the faith of the fathers of Nicaea and Ephesus.[15] The appeal to the fathers which is also suggested by this document is not in fact instrumental, if like them we think that it supports the idea of an inadequacy of theological concepts, suggesting among other things recourse to a plurality of images to avoid the risk of a unilateral formulation of the content of faith. Even in the greatest heat of conflict it is possible to find pointers in this direction, present in undifferentiated form in the theologians of opposed camps. This is shown, for example, on the one hand by the Monophysite Philoxenus of Mabbug (died 523) and on the other by the Nestorian Babai the Great (died c. 628).[16] For both, in fact any image or metaphor used to express the mystery of the incarnation can only illustrate one of its aspects; so these must not be used exclusively, but with an awareness of their partial usefulness, and along with others.

The contemporary exponents of dialogue are thus profiting from these indications, which are inculcating a renewed sense of the transcendence and impenetrability of the mystery of the divine condescension towards humankind.[17] Thus they continue to drink from that patristic spring on whose vital force these churches have drawn over the course of centuries. The topicality of this legacy, and the ecumenical potential which it contains, can also be confirmed from other perspectives: with renewed attention to the specificity of individual liturgical traditions, more closely linked with the period of origins;[18] or with the commitment to be inspired even more deeply by the apostolic kerygma and the common legacy of the councils in the enunciation of the faith. Here priority is given to methods of recognizing the distinct, albeit partial, value of those councils which were not received by some churches, like the Council of Ephesus for the 'Nestorians' and the Council of Chalcedon for the 'Monophysites'.[19] This revisiting of the individual ecclesial fragments of the Christian East could therefore focus on a reconstitution of unity, provided that this is conceived of in a pluralistic and fraternal form, capable of safeguarding the riches and varieties of individual communities, which are to find peace with one another through a spirit of communion, and animated (as the Vienna declaration recommends) by the 'compassion of God'.

Translated by Mortimer Bear

Notes

1. See Hegel's criticism of the 'repellent spectre of particularities in dogmatic lucubrations', quoted by P. Kawerau, 'Allgemeine Kirchengeschichte und Ost-kirchengeschichte', *Zeitschrift für Religions- und Geistesgeschichte* 14, 1962, 309. This was taken up by A. von Harnack (*Lehrbuch der Dogmengeschichte* II, Tübingen [5]1931, 438–9), for whom Eastern Christianity had become a kind of 'religion of the amulet, the fetish and magic, on which the dogmatic spectrum, Jesus Christ, oscillated'.

2. A. Böhlig, 'Der christliche Orient als weltgeschichtliches Problem', *Zeitschrift für Religions- und Geistesgeschichte* 17, 1965, 97–114.

3. Bat Ye'or, *Les Chrétientés d'Orient entre Jihad et Dhimmitude. VIe-XXe siècle*, Paris 1991.

4. For the two series of common features see respectively J-P. Valgones, *Vie et mort des chrétiens d'Orient. Des origines à nos jours*, Paris 1994, 150ff. and J. Leory, 'Les

églises orientales non orthodoxes', in H. C. Puech (ed.), *Histoire des religions* II, Paris 1972, 869–910.

5. E. Cerulli, 'L'oriente cristiano nell' unità delle sue tradizioni', in *L'oriente cristiano nella storia della civiltà. Atti del convegno internazionale. Accademia Nazionale dei Lincei*, Rome 1964, 9–43. Forms of interaction in the *lex orandi* are also represented by the rich religious hymnography, which overcomes confessional barriers, as has happened among the various churches in the area of Syria (cf. I.-H. Dalmais, 'Die nichtbyzantinischen orientalischen Liturgien', in *Handbuch der Ostkirchenkunde* II, ed. W. Nyssen, H.-J. Schulz and P. Wierz, Düsseldorf 1985, ²1989, 101–27, esp. 103ff.).

6. Among other things M. van Esbroeck, 'Les églises orientales non syriennes', *Le Muséon* 106, 1993, 97–117 connects the very title Catholicos, used to indicate the greatest ecclesiastical authority in some Eastern churches, with Jerusalem. The link with Jerusalem has been vital not only for the churches of the Caucasus (Armenia and Georgia) but also for the Abyssinian church (E. Cerulli, *Etiopi in Palestina. Storia della comunità etiopica di Gerusalemme* [2 vols], Rome 1943–1947).

7. Cf. the text of the *Synodicon Orientale* ed. J.-B. Chabot, Paris 1902, quoted by Mar Bawai Soro, 'La formule christologique de Vienne dans la perspective assyrienne', *Istina* 40, 1995, 21.

8. As H.-J. Schulz, 'Die Ostkirchen: Begriff und überlieferungsgeschichtliche Bedeutung', in *Handbuch der Ostkirchenkunde* (n. 5), points out, the autocephalic approach goes back to the norm of the apostolic constitutions. According to Canon 34, the bishops of all nations are to know that it is the first among them and must be considered as its head.

9. Even in the fourteenth century, Abidsho refers to the cornerstone of the patriarchates to justify the basically autonomous, but not separate, existence of the Eastern church over against the universal church (S. Jammo, 'Three Synods of the Church of the East and their Two Ecclesiologies', in *Syriac Dialogue. First Non-Official Consultation on Dialogue within the Syriac Tradition*, Vienna 1994, 87–95).

10. Down to our day the most notable case is that of the Armenian church, but on a historical level the role of the laity has been brought out, for example, for the Western Syrian Church by B. Spuler, 'Die West-syrische (monophysitische) Kirche unter dem Islam', *Saeculum* 9, 1958, 322–44, esp. 335.

11. J. M. Fiey, '"Rùm" a l'est de l'Euphrate', *Le Muséon* 90, 1977, 365–420, recalls from among the precursors of a similar 'ecumenical' attitude the figure of Abu 'Ali Nazif bn Yumn, a Melkite, priest, philosopher and doctor in tenth-century Baghdad and author of a treatise on the unity of Christians, in which he argued that the Christian gifts, whatever their confession, did not differ on the significance of the union of the natures, though adopting different formulae (399).

12. Cf. B. L. Zekiyan, 'Riflessioni preliminari sulla spiritualità armena. Una cristianità di "frontera" martyria ed apertura all oikoumene', *Orientalia Christiana Periodica* 61, 1995, 335–65, esp. 356ff.

13. For this assessment, with particular reference to the modern era, see Valgones, *Vie et mort des chrétiens d'Orient* (n. 4), 157.

14. See W. Hage, 'Kulturelle Kontakte des ostsyrischen Christentums in Zentralasien', in *III Symposium Syriacum 1980. Les contacts du monde syriaque avec les autres cultures*, ed. R. Lavenant, Rome 1983, 143–59. Cf. P. Kawerau, 'Zur Kirchengeschichte Asiens', in *Stat crux dum volvitur orbis. FS H. Lilje*, ed. G. Hoffman and K. H. Rengstorf, Berlin 1959, 68–76.

15. See the text in A. Stirnemann, 'Le dialogue de Vienne entre théologiens

catholiques et pré-chalcédoniens et l'étude menée sur Nestorius et le nestorianisme', *Istina* 40, 1995, 1.

16. Cf. Philoxenus of Mabbug, *Tractatus tres* (SCSCO Scr.Syr.9), 152–5, and Babai the Great, *Liber de unione* (CSCO, SCr.Syr.34), 233f. and the remarks by S. Brock, 'The Church of the East in the Sasasanian Empire up to the Sixth Century and its Absence from the Councils in the Roman Empire', in *Syriac Dialogue* (n. 9), 83–4.

17. See for example the position taken by Mar Bawai Soro, 'La formule christologi-que' (n. 7), 10–11, for whom the awareness of the inadequacy of any definition of faith is the premise for accepting a pluralism of dogmatic formulations; within this perspective it is possible to reconstitute the breaks between Chalcedonianism, 'Monophysites' and 'Nestorians'.

18. This is the case with the Anaphora of Addi and Mari (cf. P. Hofrichter, 'The Anaphora of Addai and Mari in the Church of the East – Eucharist without Institution Narrative?', in *Syriac Dialogue* [n. 9], 182–91).

19. Cf. E. Lane, 'Ein christologischer Konsensus zwischen der katholischen Kirche und den orientalisch-orthodoxen Kirchen', in *Chalzedon und die Folgen*, Innsbruck and Vienna 1992, 421–32.

Heresies in the Middle Ages: 'There are Two Churches'

Anne Brenon

The notion of heresy implies that of a militant orthodoxy. It was current in the long period of the development of a Catholic orthodoxy, issuing, under imperial pressure, in the councils of Nicaea (325) and Constantinople (381). After the triumph of this orthodoxy over the great heresies of early Christianity, the concept of heresy seemed to disappear from people's minds. The last person to be executed for heresy in the Latin West was Priscillian, the ascetic bishop of Avila, who was condemned and decapitated in 384. It was not until the year 1000, the dawn of the romance period and feudalism with its three orders, that the figure of the heretic reappeared. In 1022, almost 700 years after the execution of Priscillian of Avila, twelve canons of Orleans Cathedral were burned alive for heresy on the orders of the Capetian Robert the Pious. This was the first stake in Christian history. It was to be followed by many others.[1]

I. The dialectic of the two churches

The heretics appear in history only when they are denounced as such. The period around the year 1000 was characterized both by spiritual renewal (under the aegis of the Reformed Benedictine order of Cluny) and eschatological anxieties (the famous 'terrors' of the year 1000, of the year 1033 and so on). The new figure of the heretic was born from the pen of the monastic clerks and chroniclers, as the false prophet predicted by the Apocalypse who would announce the Antichrist; the heretic was the agent of evil whom the Clunian – later Cistercian – monk and Christian knight had to fight here on earth.

Suffice it to say that the phenomenon of heresy was again associated with a certain militant conception of the church, of the kind that was to issue in the spirit of the Crusades. Before the infidels, strictly speaking, it was within Christianity itself that those who were to be excluded were identified, with the features of sorcerers and demons, and the names of heretics, ministers of the devil, Manichaeans or apostles of Satan. In the undergrowth of eleventh-century texts, poor but pointed, the historian can in fact see communities of men and women, a mixture of clergy, religious and lay people, calling for a return to the ideals of the primitive church and claiming to follow the discipline of the apostles and the sole law of the gospel.[2] In their appeals to the gospel, the most ardent of these communities embarked on the way of dissidence: in other words, disobedience to and criticism of Rome.

In the time of a rich and established church, one can see them mocking the superstitious practices which it encourages: the cult of relics, crucifixes and images. They reject all that seems to them to be a later addition to the bare message of the New Testament, from the baptism of small children to the Roman hierarchy. Claiming to be followers of the apostles, these dissidents simply call themselves Christians, apostles, or Christ's poor. Since they probably represent the strongest ferment of the spiritual quest of their time, they crystallize the person of the heretic.

It is clear that the church writers of the eleventh century do not denounce the irruption of 'Manichaeans' in their world because they fear that Europe would be subjected to an invasion of Manichaeans from a doubtful East, but because the apocalyptic and monastic spirituality of the time is itself, as Georges Duby put it, 'totally Manichaean', haunted by the fight between the archangel and the dragon. It is only in a contrast with the image of the legions of the dragon that the monks, rivalled by the heretics, can claim to be angelic figures in the enclosed light of their abbeys, from which they mean to bring order to society in a hierarchy by divine right. For a long time Christian ideology was to feed on this dualistic vision of the necessary combat of good (which is defending itself) against evil (which is attacking).[3]

The dialectic of mediaeval heresy seems to be that Western Christianity burns those whom it excludes but who claim to be true Christians – and they call themselves true Christians because the world burns them; because the world persecutes them as it persecuted Christ and his apostles. They use the New Testament, and particularly the Gospel and First Letter of John, a great deal to contrast their church of God, consisting of the gentle and the meek, with the church of the world, the Roman church which persecutes them; whereas the Gregorian Roman church claims to be the sole legitimate heir of the church of Peter, the catholic and apostolic church exposed to the treacherous hypocrisy of the false prophets of the Antichrist.

II. The persecution of heresy: from the crusade to the Inquisition

Thanks to a relatively precise series of documents, the historian can trace from the heart of the heresies of the year 1000 the emergence of a real Christian counter-church. This was immediately denounced and repressed, but it was organized in clandestine fashion from the first half of the twelfth century as a religious order around bishops who had the power to ordain and to absolve from sins. Rejecting the authority of the papacy, it claimed authentic descent from the apostles and claimed for its clergy (which was mixed) the honourable name of Christian. The term 'Cathars' (a learned word-play on 'pure' and 'a sorcerer who worships the cat') which was given to the heretical communities in 1163 by Eckbert of Schönau, a cleric in the Rhineland, is the normal designation for them today.[4]

Pursued from Flanders to the Rhineland, from Champagne to Burgundy, betrayed everywhere to the episcopal courts, imprisoned and burned and soon eliminated, these Cathars enjoyed a respite in Languedoc during the second half of the twelfth century and the first years of the thirteenth. There, as in the Ghibelline cities of Italy or in the kingdom of Bosnia, they were tolerated by the great princes and supported by their vassals. So they were able to give structure to their churches and dioceses, establish regular houses for their order, and engage in evangelization without fear of repression. They could also produce liturgical rituals and theological treatises, some of which have come down to us.

Pope Innocent III (1198–1216), a champion of pontifical theocracy and himself a great lawyer, succeeded in completing the arsenal of canon law for repressing heretics: he went so far as to liken heresy to the crime of lèse-majesté towards God. Proclaiming the plenitude of the power of the Holy See over the European kingdoms, he reorganized Western Christianity at the Lateran Council of 1215, as a community of the faithful, strictly defined by its creed and by its parochial and confessional framework. Those who did not conform, those who were excluded, i.e. at that time the heretics, were rejected as being in outer darkness and eternal damnation, symbolized by the stake.

By the same logic, Innocent III completed the development of the concept of the holy war, calling for a crusade in Christian lands, the crusade against the Albigensians. From 1209 to 1229 a crusade, which was first a crusade of barons and then a royal crusade against the great princes and feudal lords of Languedoc who were guilty of tolerating heresy, resulted in the attachment of Languedoc to the crown of France (the seneschalsy of Carcassone/Béziers, then in 1271 the seneschalsy of Toulouse) and the elimination of those princely lines which had been protectors of heresy. From now on the hands of the papacy were free to act.

The Inquisition, a procedure of enquiry into the crime of heresy, which did not depend on the pope alone and was entrusted to the new Mendicant Orders, was replaced from 1233 by ordinary tribunals held by the bishops.

Founded on the principle of compulsory general confession, the Inquisition played a precise penitential role aimed at the absolution and reconciliation to the Roman church of all the populations of the south; lumping confession, deposition and informing together, it invented the modern police investigation, with the aim of depriving heresy of its pastors, who from now on were clandestine, and destroying the networks which gave it solidarity. This was achieved in Languedoc in the first half of the fourteenth century. Paradoxically, the registers of depositions and the sentences handed out by the Inquisition are now a documentary source of the first order about Catharism in Languedoc.

Created with the aim of annihilating the Cathar counter-church and reconciling all the people of Languedoc in the one faith and order of the Roman Catholic Church, the Inquisition, backed up by the theological works of Dominican doctors – and soon by Thomism – was used before the end of the thirteenth century to uproot other tendencies towards religious disorder.

The effectiveness of the Inquisition against the Waldensian movement, which had a less rigid structure than the Cathar church and as a result was more fitted to clandestine survival, was only relative. Spread throughout Western Europe from the first years of the twelfth century, the claim to gospel poverty and free preaching of the Word of God crystallized from the 1170s around the vocation of Peter Valdes of Lyons, whom the intransigence of the religious authorities drove progressively first into schism and then into heresy. The Waldensian movement, the Poor of Lyons and then the Poor Lombards, which prefigured the birth of the Mendicants at the beginning of the thirteenth century and particularly Franciscanism, became more radical as a result of the mediaeval persecutions; it spread towards Central Europe, rallying first to the Hussites and then to the Protestant Reformation in 1532.[5]

The Waldensians rejected the authoritarian structures of the Roman hierarchy and challenged the validity of the sacraments administered by the unworthy hands of its clergy. In the middle of the thirteenth century a radical wing was formed by the Spiritual Franciscans, who claimed to be faithful to the model of St Francis, and denounced both the tendency of their Order to become monastic and its involvement in the repression of the Inquisition. Supported in Languedoc by their third order of Beguines and Beghards, they progressively adopted the prophetic visions of the Joachimites – more or less direct heirs of Joachim of Fiore – and announced the imminence of a church of the Holy Spirit destined to obliterate the dominance of the all too material Roman church, with its violence and opulence. Then the era of the Son would give place to that of the Spirit. In Italy, the movement of the Apostolici begun by Gerard Segarelli and Fra Dolcino formed the revolutionary paroxysm of these religious movements claiming to be the church of the Spirit and calling for justice in this world.[6]

In the first decades of the fourteenth century the Inquisition sent the Spirituals and the Beguines in Languedoc to the stake as it did the Apostolici in Italy; at the same time the last Cathars were burned, as in England were John Wyclif and his Lollards. Rather later, John Huss and then the Taborites suffered the same fate in Bohemia, in their turn linking the imperatives of a moral and theological reform of a perverted church with those of social justice.

In general, throughout the Middle Ages, the dialectic of the two churches, opposing papacy to heretics, represented a claim to belong to the authentic church of Christ and the apostles. The logic of the militant church led the Roman church to the ideology of the crusade and the practice of the Inquisition. In the Gothic period, Spiritual Franciscans and Apostolici set their faith in the advent of a spiritual church against the material church which was in place. In the Romance period, the Cathar church had claimed to incarnate it. Fragmentation in the name of a quest for unity? We find this *Leitmotif* for two centuries in Cathar preaching: 'There are two churches: one flees and forgives (Matt. 10.22–23); the other possesses and burns.'[7]

Translated by John Bowden

Notes

1. Robert Moore, *The Formation of a Persecuting Society. Power and Deviance in Western Europe, 950–1250*, Oxford 1987.

2. Pierre Bonassie and Richard Landes, 'Une nouvelle hérésie est née dans le monde', in *Les sociétés méridionales autour de l'An Mil . . .*, Paris 1992, 435–59.

3. Anne Brenon, 'Les hérésies de l'An Mil. Nouvelles perspectives sur les origines du catharisme', *Heresis* 24, 1995, 21–36.

4. For Catharism in general and the persecution of it, see Jean Duvernoy, *Le catharisme*, Toulouse: *1. La Religion des cathares*, 1976; *2. L'Histoire des cathares*, 1979, revised edition by Anne Brenon, *Les cathares: vie et mort d'une Eglise chrétienne*, Paris 1996.

5. For Waldensianism in general see Jean Gonet and Amadeo Molnar, *Les Vaudois au Moyen Age*, Turin 1974.

6. There is a good synthesis on these movements in Grado Giovanni Merlo, *Eretici ed Eresie medievali*, Bologna 1989, 99–128.

7. Quoted several times, from the mouth of the preacher Pierre Authié, in the *Registre d'Inquisition de Jacques Fournier (1318–1325)*, ed. Jean Duvernoy (3 vols.), Toulouse 1965. Compare the words which Evervin of Steinfeld attributes to the Cathars of the Rhineland in 1143, in his letter to Saint Bernard. For this point see Brenon, *Les cathares* (n. 4), esp. 50–1.

Why Did Jansenism Want 'Catholicity' for Itself?

Bernard Plongeron

Because it was one, yet multiple, in the period of the seventeenth and eighteenth centuries and in Europe – it would be better to speak of it in the plural – Jansenism can support every interpretation: 'heresy', 'sect' (in his *Inconvénients d'État procédant du jansénisme* of 1654 Marandé, the king's adviser, makes it 'a sect of the State rather than of religion'), not to mention schism (the support of the French Jansenists for the church of Utrecht in its break with Rome in the eighteenth century). It could even be seen as a populist break with a miraculous and 'prophetic' character in the convulsive crisis, with actions that ranged from eccentricities around the tomb of the deacon Pâris at Saint-Médard Cemetery in Paris (1727–1732) to the strange foundation of a 'Republic of Jesus Christ' by Curé Bonjour and some of the visionaries in the region of Lyons (Forez) after the French Revolution.

Jansenism is usually thought to be related to an Augustinian school of theology, centred on the problem of grace – which it in fact was at the time of Port-Royal and Pascal. After 1650 it is seen as a movement and then, after the affair of the bull *Unigenitus* (1713), as a 'patriotic' party opposed to the absolutist state and against all religious, political and economic 'despotisms'. Indeed it was one of the first to give a practical sense to the term 'despotism', borrowed from Montesquieu. It is thought of as an anti-Jesuit block, as a united front against all the Ultramontane pretensions of the 'Court of Rome'; and it is seen as opposing its 'Catholicity' both to the Calvinist Protestants and to the Enlightenment 'philosophes' with whom in fact it has some connections. The spectrum of opinions and standpoints among the Jansenists is a wide one: from the rigorists to the 'centrists' or 'third party'. In every case, throughout its rich and tumultuous history, including its Reformist action towards the France of Louis XV and the Europe of Joseph II, despite the splits within the Jansenist nebulas (those directly affiliated and the sympathizers), one basic intuition is a constant: the need to forge a political ethic for a world fundamentally corrupted by sin, either to reject that world (which was Port-Royal's theological option) or to transform it by re-injecting into it the ideas of the primitive church (poverty and 'universal' consensus through elections within the civil and religious hierarchies). This latter was the project of practical theology which historians call the 'political' Jansenism of the eighteenth century.

This relationship between Jansenism and politics is invariably based on the ethical principle according to which good customs (according to the post-Tridentine scheme of *fides et mores*; in this event *verae mores ex bona fide*) are called acquired virtues, indispensable for the life of a state. Now in the eyes of the Jansenists, all acts necessarily proceed from charity or concupiscence: the acquired virtues deriving from this 'middle faculty' which is corrupt reason are themselves the fruit of concupiscence. Since their principle is bad, they have to be proscribed.

> Here we touch on the very essence of relations between Jansenism and the world order: if the reasonable acts and customs which are the foundation of all social life are alien to charity, some Jansenists will draw the logical conclusion of a total rejection of the world.[1]

That was the spirit in Port-Royal, in the middle of the seventeenth century, a community of solitaries whom Louis XIV, according to Saint-Simon, called 'republicans'. We should understand the word in its old sense, without the slightest allusion to a form of political regime. Port-Royal is a life-style within a small republic of independent spirits sworn to a 'hidden' existence, to rural solitude. In this way Port-Royal makes a living protest against the hierarchical and sumptuous world of the monarchy of Louis XIV and its 'despotic' soliciting of consciences by the attraction of 'talents' – Port-Royal is full of them. It is a protest against royal bureaucracy, the cost of which enrages the rising bourgeoisie; and finally it is a protest against the encouragement of capitalism, the triumph of greed and symbol of corruption. At that time the Port-Royal protest broke with Calvinism, which, through the process illuminated by Max Weber, leads to a concentration of riches. Jansenism proved to be more haughty about the Catholic tradition – contrary to the laxity of the Jesuits – in affirming a business ethic. The tricky problem of credit was one of the first matters of conscience which arose from the Jansenists and divided them among themselves as well as dividing France from Holland, depending on the reading of the scholastic bans on loans at interest.

For a long time the northern provinces had based their prosperity on commerce and credit: the current practice was a contract involving bonds redeemable on both sides, i.e. repayable on demand by either the creditor or the debtor. In 1658 the states had approved these financial practices and declared that they were totally dependent on the civil power. Could the Catholics, who were numerous in Holland but simply tolerated, rebel against this state policy? A number of Louvain theologians (including Jean Opstraët) sought to calm their scruples, fortified by the Jansenist support for the 'movement', to which Pascal and Arnauld gave timid backing. The great majority of Jansenists formed the 'resistance': hostile to any form of Protestant contagion, they reinforced the rigour of the scholastic bans in the face of Colbert's mercantilism and speculations on the exchange under the system set up by John Law, at the time of the regency. Furthermore, lending at interest and a credit policy became practices accepted in the church of Utrecht.

In this way terms like 'movement', 'resistance' and then 'middle party' appeared. These broke up the Jansenist movement in the name of moral practice and a greater Catholic orthodoxy: the fiercer Augustinians did not hesitate to resort to the School in its defence. Perhaps the differences would have been even more numerous had not the affair of the bull *Unigenitus* reconstituted the logic of the Jansenist rejection on new foundations, at the turn between two centuries which had contrasting values. Through its theologians and moralists, the seventeenth century was intent on constructing a Christian policy on the basis of reasons of state. The eighteenth century opened the period of a crisis of authority in the apparatus of state and church under the impact of individualism which was denounced for its spirit of free examination, and in the judgment of the ecclesiastical hierarchy was a factor in irreligion, though it was celebrated for its fight on behalf of the rights of conscience. The emergence of citizens' rights under the slogan of 'reasonable religion' was also a factor in this impact; this was the *rationabile obsequium* prescribed by Paul in Romans 12, without which the submission to the civil powers in the famous Romans 13 becomes incomprehensible or totally false. The Jansenists largely became involved in this 'individualism' which prefigured the Catholic Enlightenment.[2] This century of the Enlightenment got caught up in the furious controversies over ecclesiology, the favourite domain of the canon lawyers who dominated the period, in the company of the apologists of the 'social utility of religion'.

According to its authors was this second or third Jansenism a branch, a 'fragmentation', as compared with the original theological project within a global Catholicism, as has sometimes been claimed? By contrast, Abbé Duguet (1649–1733), a moderate Jansenist, showed how the transition between the two centuries came about and why tradition and modernity were far from being opposites. He first expounded his ecclesiology as professor of positive theology at the Oratorian seminary of Saint-Magloire.

His *Conférences ecclésiastiques* (1678–1679) led him to discuss the tricky point of discipline in the primitive church, the absolute point of reference. The development of discipline in the Catholic tradition, which could be deplored for its decadence, should not, in his view, put in question a total love of the 'infallibility' of the universal church.

> The church could not have been infallible, or would have ceased to be so, had it once regarded as truths what it would now regard as excesses. It is we who have changed . . . On the contrary, nothing should give us so much love for it, so much devotion, so much respect as to see to what it has descended for us. But at the same time we must be confused, we must have been so sick that we have not been able to endure the remedies, and have only been able to be cured by the weakening and relaxation of discipline.

As an intermediary between this world and the world beyond, for Duguet as for Arnauld the church is involved in a dialectic between the stable time of immutable truth and linear time, the finitude of human beings steeped in increasing corruption. The corruption of temporality cannot touch the intemporality of doctrine:

> If it would be a crime to regard the church fathers as cruel and impudent, it would be an equally great crime to regard today's church as lax and having abandoned the truths which it had once supported: *Jesus Christi heri et hodie, ipse et in saecula* (Heb. 13.8).[3]

It is by virtue of this dogmatic conviction that Duguet outlines the plan of the ideal Christian city throughout a work which enjoyed tremendous success. This was *Institution d'un prince*, composed around 1699, but published only in 1739 to the applause of Saint-Simon and the Marquis of Argenson. Duguet's system is original in two ways. Not only does he not even mention the problem of the acceptance or rejection of the world, but as a premise to any political consideration he posits the possibility of a Christian order, the conditions of which the prince is bound to offer to his subject. As Saint-Beuve felt strongly in the case of other Jansenists, Duguet is sustaining a paradox which is hardly more astonishing in our day: it is from his basic pessimism, a 'disenchantment' with the world, that his need to organize the world arises. Who would not find to be of the utmost topicality his sense of the media, which led him to found the first popular journal, *Les Nouvelles Ecclésiastiques*, which through a system of correspondents was to provide immediate, abundant, international information? Here was a real 'party' organ, the venomous comments of which were formidable and feared. Who could forget its technical precision on economic questions, the problems of the treasury, savings, politics, industrialization, and above all its diagnoses of the ravages of capitalism and solutions for full employment?

Far from excluding the world, Duguet planted Jansenism at the heart of Catholicity, whose monarchical tradition and Gallicanism he espoused, drawing the last consequences from them. He avoids the Reformist prudery which makes the political success of a number of his friends mixed up in Richérist theses defend corporatism: for example, the syndicates of priests which formed against the bishops, from the Dauphiné to Brittany, to defend both their institution by divine right and their standard of living. Like Bossuet, Duguet thinks that the king is in the image of God, to the point of having a mission to perfect the temporal order without encroaching upon the spiritual, the domain of the church. This is an elegant way of proclaiming the distinction between the two powers, dear to all Jansenists. He shares Catholic integralism, sustained by the party devoted to the seventeenth century, which limited the power of the king by his own conscience as a man and as a Christian. That is why Bossuet, like the Jansenists, exalted the monarchy by divine right but stigmatized the practical policy of absolutism which since Louis XIV was only its usurped form. The monarchy by divine right is one of the 'great institutions' which deserve absolute respect, and the exercising of monarchical power is one of the 'natural greatnesses', which call for critical examination and exhaust themselves before the sphere reserved for the individual conscience.

By an interpretation which was bold for its time, Duguet, like a number of Jansenists of the 'third party', argued from Romans 13 the right to resist passively if it was necessary to preserve a religion and the rights of the conscience. In the same way civil disobedience entered political ethics and immediately applied itself to the distinction between 'fact' and 'right' in connection with a formula which radicalized the position. We know that the famous bull *Unigenitus Dei filius* of 8 September 1713, promulgated at the request of Louis XIV, condemned 101 propositions extracted from the text of the *Réflexions morales* of the Oratorian Quesnel. Just think of what was at stake ecclesiologically when proposition 91 in particular was censured!

> The fear even of an unjust excommunication must never prevent us from doing our duty. One never leaves the church, even when it seems that one has been banished by human wickedness, when one is attached to God, to Jesus Christ and to the church itself by love (John 9.23).

Leave the church? There could be no question of that for all the appellants of the bull: around 3,000 out of 100,000 French ecclesiastics, definitively excommunicated by Clement IX in 1718, fifteen of them bishops exiled in their diocese by the king. A resolute minority and proud of being so, they emphasized their communion with the universal church to escape the phenomenon of sectarianism, and worked actively and openly in every area of influence, mainly the bourgeoisie of the Parliaments, who also had accounts to settle with royal absolutism. Precisely because they were in a minority, they regarded themselves as the salt of Catholicity, according to a vision of the church, the strategy of which was defined by one of the most extreme of the appelants, the theologian Besoigne, in his *Catéchisme pour les temps de trouble* (1733):

> I have said that there are functions of the church which presuppose a universal consent and a moral unanimity, like the function of deciding on challenges to the faith; and there are others which can be performed by a small number, like teaching certain truths, conserving the deposit of the tradition, living in love, groaning and praying, worshipping God in spirit and in truth.

Thus the church is like the life of the human body (or any body politic): the union of all the parts is necessary for health, but the body 'is always thought to be alive when there is more than one part of the body which is not dead'.

There is no doubt that from then on the Jansenists regarded themselves as the *ultima pars* which had become the *sanior pars* of a church with gangrene, as of the state ravaged by royal absolutism. And since for them the church was in the state, although they are distinct powers, by the same token political regeneration was the task of the church. Their theological and political primitivism led them to celebrate a 'national religion' in the struggles of the eighteenth century. In a constitutional monarchy like that of 1791, the purified church would be given a public status in which all functions, both civil and religious, were subject to election, and thus to 'universal content' by democratic means. We all too often forget that the 1790 Civil Constitution of the Clergy, developed by the canon lawyers of the Comité Ecclésiastique, is only a device within the French Constitution of 1791. It was in thinking of the advent of this democratic age that the very Jansenist Camus, one of the kingpins of the Civil Constitution of the Clergy, evoked before his colleagues of the Constitutive Assembly in September 1789 the 'priesthood of the baptized' for implementing the *rationabile obsequium*.

That was the supreme paradox of this Jansenism which was in process of disappearing on the threshold of the French Revolution. This minority movement, which did not enjoy any official role in the church and the state, engaged in increasingly effective lobbying between 1760 and 1770 through the multiplicity of its networks: press, lawyers, polemists and an international chain of bishops in quest of ecclesiastical reforms. While maintaining their particular Augustinian character, the Jansenists succeeded in being at the cross-roads of different oppositions, at the focal point of all the combats for the rights of conscience and 'God's cause'. In the turbulence of the ideas of the time they exercised the real power of tribunes through the ardour of their campaigns (the suppression of the Jesuits), the power of their learning and the rigour of their theological convictions, which contrasted with the surrounding confusion, the damaging climate of the universities, and a papacy which had been seriously weakened since the reign of Benedict XIV.

For all that, recent historiography has ceased to make Jansenism the cause of the Revolution, while emphasizing its work of undermining the absolutist Ancien Régime. On the other hand, more recent research has shown how much the Jansenists contributed to a new political culture:

> There are numerous parallels between political organization and ecclesiastical order at this time: a church with a Richérist inspiration and a democratic state are based on the will of the community which designates some individuals for dogmatic or disciplinarian functions.[4]

The influence of Jansenism on the structures of the constitutional church remains more controversial. It is true that we can note convergences during the reorganization after the Terror; these are largely due to the responsibility of the laity particularly in holding diocesan and metropolitan synods between 1796 and 1802. Does that mean that Abbé Grégoire was a Jansenist? That would be to open up another debate . . . [5]

Notes

1. R. Taveneaux, *Jansenisme et Politique*, Paris 1965, 16 (a basic reference work).
2. B. Plongeron, *Théologie et Politique au siècle des Lumières (1770–1820)*, Geneva 1973. For the implications of the *rationabile obsequium* in the European culture of the eighteenth century see 105–6, 280–5, 312–21.
3. F. Vanhoorne, 'Du jansénisme au mercantilisine: la politique de l'abbé du Guet', *Revue d'Histoire Ecclésiastique* XCI, 1996, 41–65.
4. F. Hildesheimer, *Le Jansénisme. L'histoire et l'héritage*, Paris 1992, 95–101; J. P. Chantin, *Le Jansénisme. Entre hérésie imaginaire et résistance catholique XVIIe-XXe siècle*, Paris 1996.
5. B. Plongeron, *L'abbé Grégoire ou l'arche de la Fraternité*, Paris 1989.

III · The Planetary Horizon

The Fragment and the Part: An Indic Reflection

Raimon Panikkar

Accepit panem et benedicens fregit (Mark 14.22)

Having to reflect on the 'fragmentation of the church' from an Asian perspective, I prefer to limit myself to an Indic viewpoint. 'Indic' stands for the traditional cultures of that subcontinent of which India is a political unit, but not the only one. We should add that the Indic mentality is not uniform either.

If Indic theology represents *in nuce* a theological mutation, as the many publications of the 'Indian Theological Association' clearly show, a theological meditation coming from that part of the world should not (subservient to the techno-scientific fashion) jump into answering the question without critically reflecting on the nature of the problem which has triggered the question itself.[1]

For too long the church, or rather the churches, in non-Western countries have been simply colonies of the 'mother' churches – not only financially but also intellectually and spiritually. 'The Basel Mission', for instance, has a sophisticated and wonderful theology, but I wonder what its impact could be on an Indic soul over against the different theology of, say, the 'Swedish Compound'. We have exported the European disputes into countries which did not see the vital connection between Christ and the theological interpretations of a past foreign to them. And now those countries begin to feel proud of being 'independent' – in spite of the flaws of that *svarâj* or self-governance.

This oversimplified introduction, which in no way wants to be a criticism of the past, offers the 'Sitz im Leben' for the overcondensed following reflections. I emphasize that we are dealing with a way of thinking and feeling which may be refractory to the premises of historical Christendom and the post-Cartesian assumptions which are, by and large, the predominant categories of modern theological interpretations of Christian faith. The necessary pre-understanding of the Christian mystery by the cultures of Asia may not lead to the same *intellectus fidei*, or the same vision of the church, in our case.

'The church in fragments.' Which church? I venture a threefold answer which may reflect an Asian view.

The church:
– as an organization is in fragments;
– as an institution is in crisis;
– as an organism is wounded.

1. An organization comes into being by an external will for some definite goal, and is maintained in its existence by a definite set of rules. It is defined by its constitution or founding charter. It needs power and a board of directors. It lives by virtue of its own efficiency. And there is no need to stress that organizations are needed for political life. Man is a political animal, a social being.

I remember Father Daniélou (at that time not yet a Cardinal) saying that what churches and sects are to the main body of Protestantism, religious orders (and congregations) are to the Catholic Church. Fragment or parts?

A 'fragment' is a 'fraction', the result of an 'infraction' we may say, playing with words, and because the church was 'fragile' it suffered a 'fracture'. A hint for historians.

A 'part' is a 'portion' of a whole and it 'participates' in it. Now, to take a part for the whole (*pars pro toto*) may be a schism if we think spatially and mechanically, but if we think symbolically and mystically it may stand for the local church (*totum in parte*). A hint for theologians.

If the church were only an organization, with a 'confederation of churches' we might have an answer to the fragmentation. But a certain theology would maintain that the fractures are so serious that they cannot be healed by a super-organization, although such a confederation may be regarded as a pragmatic way of dealing with the problem. It may not be foreign to the genius of the Anglo-Saxon mentality to find a practical answer in a 'World Council of Churches' – other ecclesiological problems notwithstanding.

2. An institution comes into being by an inner necessity of communal life. It is a cultural phenomenon. Man is a cultural animal. It requires a certain accepted structure. It needs a certain recognized order which crystallizes in a moral code. *Leges mori serviunt* (laws are subservient to custom), the Western classics said. Caste, marriage and state are institutions. They are alive because of the need felt by those who belong to them – or because of sheer inertia for a time being.

Institutions are needed, although they should be flexible enough to fulfil their function of enhancing human life. Life is the ground for *dharma*, says the Hitopadesha (I, 37). *Dharma* is closer to nature than to law, to order than to duty.

There is no doubt that the church as an institution is in crisis. 'Christianity yes, churchianity no', say many people in India. The crisis has many causes. I shall mention only two of them.

One is the imbalance between the modern mentality (with all its ambivalence) and the traditional ecclesial worldview (with all its richness).

An optimistic interpretation of the crisis is what the late Cardinal Suhard of Paris called a 'crisis of growth', an opinion shared also by Pope John XXIII. Modern society, for good and/or ill, has evolved at a pace which has not been the rhythm of the church. Thousands of books have been written on the subject. It concerns the church at large, it rebounds on Asia, but it is not particularly an Eastern problem. In spite of the over 200 million Asian Christians, theology is still mainly a Western concern – as the very name 'theology' betrays.

From an also still optimistic perspective the second origin of the crisis may be called a crisis of adaptation, like the crisis an adopted adolescent from an Indian village can have when transplanted into a Western family. There is no doubt that the church, some historical exceptions notwithstanding, is a Western institution transplanted into the East when it was practically sixteen centuries old and already had a strongly developed constitution. No wonder that many a trauma did appear in the last centuries.

One way of minimizing the scars was to keep Christians aloof from the main currents of the cultural and political life of the respective countries. One could call it ghetto mentality, compound syndrome, superiority complex, other-worldly attitude, and the like. The theological temptation was, of course, to justify this policy by affirming that 'we' had the whole truth, were better, and 'Catholic'; in short, a theology on which nowadays we would put the label of 'exclusivism'.

But with the decolonization of the world those churches (many of them still under 'Propaganda fidei') want to have their say and feel they have the right and duty to affirm their Christian identity in a different manner. The inclination of many modern theologians here is towards 'inculturation' and 'inclusivism'. Much has been discussed on those issues also. I am resisting the temptation to enter that field again. Instead I wish to tackle here the Indic 'view-point' by not dealing with theological doctrines, but stressing the different ways of thinking of an important part of the Asian peoples. For brevity's sake let us elaborate on this issue, focussing on our particular point by a couple of examples.

'An Asian view' of the situation of the church today perceives the ordinary theological explanation that Jesus Christ founded an institution as exaggerated, to say the least, and it does not resonate too well in many Western theological discussions (number of sacraments, marriage rules, women priests, liturgical laws, etc.) based on arguments like the will of the founder, the translatability of the message of the Gospels into paragraphs of canon law, the theological weight of historical customs, the importance given to 'specific differences', etc. – without now taking sides or saying that one could not strike compromises and follow middle ways.

Perhaps because of the caste system ingrained in the Indic psyche or for other reasons, the fact is that the bundle of religions called Hinduism from the outside ('Hinduism' is a notion foreign to the traditional 'religions' of the Indian subcontinent) does 'function' without any notion of church as a central or even necessary institution for the existence of the religious faith and the religious life of the people.[2]

What appears in the West as 'fragments' of a church of Christ torn apart appears to the Indic mind rather as 'parts', portions of a whole whose cohesion and unity lies elsewhere, beyond any institution. Except for the Islamic mentality, the Indic soul tends to see differences as parts of a whole which does not need to be articulated in any clear and distinct idea, nor in an institutionalized way. The access to the whole is not through the sum, neither is it through the integral calculus of its parts. Were it not for the cautions and prohibitions of the Christian churches, the Eastern peoples would be prone to participate in other religious rituals as parts of a mysterious or numinous reality. They do not feel separated.

In Japan, for instance, it is not an exception to be initiated in a Shinto temple at birth, while at the same time being a practising Buddhist and nowadays even celebrating marriage in a Christian church – superficialities and eclecticisms notwithstanding. It is well known that when the Pope came to India, thousands of Hindus were keen on receiving the eucharist, without any sense of being 'fragmented' from that religious manifestation of the sacred. Not only does the church appear in portions, but religions also are seen as portions of that human dimension which in the West is called religion. One may codify *dharma*, for instance, but not institutional-ize it.

3. An organism is born; it is enlivened by a soul or living principle. It comes into existence by a fecundation between the parents. It needs health. It is not just political but natural, not just an expedient way of orderly living, but a given fact. Man is a living being. A living being is an organism, ultimately a miracle. Was the church founded or born? *Ecclesia ab Abel.*

Nobody can serve two masters. Either the church is *to mysterion tou kosmou, sacramentum mundi*, the continuation of the incarnation, the eucharist (in the sense in which the late Cardinal de Lubac expanded in his *Méditation sur l'Eglise*), and Christianity the religion of the Word (and not of the Book), or the church is not only in fragments, but is lifeless and has lost its soul – which traditionally is said to be the Holy Spirit. In fact, the people of India and other parts of Asia understand better and relate much more easily to the mystery of Easter and the eucharist than to the events of Christmas – although it all hangs together (as the Hindu, Taoist, Shinto and Buddhist minds spontaneously believe).

We cannot deny that in today's predominant culture those theologumena are practically dead or ineffective. They are reserved for mystics or holy people. After centuries of historical Christianity starting with Constantine, perhaps Torquemada is still needed, and Dostoyevsky's Grand Inquisitor has a point. But must the seed of Christ still alive in the Church be identified with the luxuriant tree of Western Christianity? And to continue with cardinals, another one of them was complaining to me, off the record, when he heard of the 'quaint' idea of Pope John that he should convene an ecumenical council: 'But who can trust in the theology of the majority of Asian and African bishops? I know only too well how rudimentary it is!' Sound advice to a board of directors before the general assembly of a corporation! Should that apply also to the church?

Far be it from me to present the Asian view as only spiritual and mystic. Nor am I saying that an *ecclesia spiritualis* can exist without a historical and an earthly incarnation. But it is also far from the intention of these lines to propose healing the wounds of the church by artificial and violent surgery. A living organism has its ways of regenerating, even if it is a fragmented bone (to follow our metaphor).

But there is still more, and this would be nearer to the Asian view. Perhaps the church is not so fragmented after all. Perhaps that Spirit of Christ, that mystical body, is well and alive, although it has escaped our control. Perhaps that Spirit which already before creation 'hovered over the waters', 'fills every creature and has knowledge of every sound' is still blowing sovereignly where 'she' wills. 'He' broke the Bread into fragments and gave it to all. Perhaps it is an urgent task to put together the broken fragments not by an external glue, but by receiving them with eucharistic reverence so as to collaborate in the redemption of the world by rebuilding the Body of Christ: to restore the dismembered body of Prajâpati, as the Veda would say.

In sum, the fact that this very language may sound strange to many ears shows already that the body of Christ is indeed wounded until the fulness of the glory is achieved.

'Which unity?' Seen from an Indic view, the unity of the church is a desperate enterprise as long as we dream of an administrative unity or a uniformity of doctrines. Man is certainly a *res cogitans*, a thinking thing, but man is much more than his ideas. Likewise, the church is much more than a belief-system. Faith is not just its intellectual articulation in beliefs – important as they are. If we *see* the church fragmented, it may be because by that name we refer only to our conception of it or to its outer garment, having dreamed of that 'seamless tunic' (John 19.23) as an image of the church. And now seeing the church torn apart by sin and time, we forget that 'He' also had other garments which were divided into four parts among Gentiles, and even that his 'type' Joseph had a 'tunic of many colours' (Gen. 37.23), as the old Christian interpretation of the *'circumdata varietate'* of the Vulgate (Ps. 44.10) shows – whatever the original text and context may be. If we see the church fragmented, it may be because we are still looking for the living among the dead and have not understood the revelation of the angel as reported by all the Synoptics: 'He is not here, he is risen.' He is to be found neither in Jerusalem nor on Gerizim, neither in Rome nor in Mecca, neither in Vrindaban or in Bodhgaya nor in Washington or Moscow, exclusively.

I should not be misunderstood. The church is also a visible society. The church of Christ subsists in the Catholic Church, said Vatican II (*Lumen gentium*, 8), acknowledging a difference between the church of Christ and the Roman church. The previous drafts were in fact amended, changing the original *est* (meaning identification) into a *subsistit in* (making room for a wider conception of church). But this 'Catholic Church', this *'ecclesia universalis'*, I would further venture to say, *exists* since the beginning of the world, *'a constitutione mundi'*, as the patristic interpretation entitles us to suggest.

I repeat that I am attempting to present an Indic view, not a theological doctrine. This view is not only an 'objective' vision; it depends mainly on the eye of the beholder. Part of the 'fragmentation' may be in our own sight. It all depends on what we see. Many an Asian Christian will understand that thousands of Europeans leave the 'church' because they do not want to contribute to a particular church-politics and thus refuse to pay church tax, but they will also think that the mystical body they belong to has little to do with Caesar's coins or the Constantinian heritage.

'We are all *brahman*', a good number of Asian people believe in different ways. But not everybody knows it (that we are *brahman*, or that we are all manifestations of an ineffable Mystery, have Buddha-nature, etc.). 'We are all Church' would be an assertion more convincing to the deep recesses of the psyche of Asian Christians – although not everybody knows it – because 'it' (*brahman*, church . . .) is a mystery. Perhaps the 'fragmentation' of the church is the great challenge for Christians in the incoming third millennium, so that the encounter with Asia and Africa may help the church to come of age. *Ecclesia semper nascitura* – 'by work and grace of the Holy Spirit'. Asian Christians have a peculiar devotion to Mary!

Notes

1. Cf. M. Amaladoss, T. K. John and G. Gispert-Sauch (ed.), *Theologizing in India*, Bangalore 1981; G. v.Leeuwen (ed.), *Searching for an Indian Ecclesiology*, Bangalore 1984.
2. Cf. some pertinent reflections in my short article 'The Hindu Ecclesial Consciousness: Some Ecclesiological Reflections', *Jeevadhara* 21, 1973, 199–205.

Latin America: Against the Threat to the Whole of Life

Paulo Suess

'Fragmentation' signalizes the destruction of the whole of life. The poor 'others' are particularly affected by this. Fragmentation is not the result of the subject-less destructive forces of modernity. It always has something to do with the claims of sectors of society and church to hegemony, and these can use both premodern and postmodern instruments (I). 'Fragmentation' in Latin America can historically be dated to the Conquista, which destroyed particular projects in the name of universality (II). In the shade of colonial conditions Christianity chased the phantom of a world in the singular and, exploiting the constellation of power, created a 'Catholic continent'. The 'Catholic unity' of Latin America began to crumble with the republican freedom of religion. Today migration dominates the scene on the market of the religions (III).

Because fragmentation must be thought of historically, becoming conscious of it can also mobilize forces for overcoming it: quests for remembrance, contextuality, communicative and social symmetry, and an articulation of solidarity (IV). Giving all subject-subject and subject-object relations a new dimension along with a complementary networking of feeling and reason, nature and spirit – in short, universality as a mosaic of whole, symmetrical and articulated parts – represents the practical horizon of this quest.

I. The problems

Global neighbourhood in the world village confronts us daily with the frontiers and the abysses between nations and cultures, social classes, generations and gender-specific groups. The globalization produced by means of communication, technology, market and capital represents a macrocultural phenomenon of levelling down, but is incapable of bringing about a world culture which can unite humankind. All over the world we lie increasingly close to one another as in an over-full prison cell; we know the planks in the eyes of others and do not want to see those in our own eyes. Latin America, too, does not love its poor migrants. Kaiová Indios from the Mato Grosso of Brazil like being taken for Japanese in the cities.

As a reaction to traumatic nearness, 'fragmentation' can be celebrated as a rite of initiation in postmodernity but also as an option for the class society, as liberation from the pressure of universal brotherhood and sisterhood. However, 'fragmentation' can be not only social irresponsibility and a narcissistic singleness but also injured talk about the 'grand narrative' of revolutionary comfort through a datable redemption which has lost its credibility. Finally, fragmentation can be a Cassandra-like cry in the face of the threatening chaos of meaningless in a multiplicity which has no points of reference; it can refer to a process of mourning which has to be undergone, to the loss of the utopian view that the life of all can be whole.

Fragmentation recalls historical conditions of violence with identifiable winners and losers. Fragments are not parts which are whole in themselves, but mutilated bodies, signs of destroyed identity, remains of a whole life. Constructing and putting together parts which are intrinsically whole and identical is an everlasting task. The awareness of fragmentariness can of itself already indicate an innovative quest for memory, context and communication, in awareness that there is a crisis. This is the significance of inculturation as a presupposition of the articulation of the different projects that are going on in these contexts. The opportunity for encounter with oneself and with others lies in reflection on identity, in shaping contextuality and in the articulation of reason which has been historically tested and is directed by experience specific to the situation.

Fragmentation in the church can quite generally be a pointer to structures of dependence which produce a contextual and historical forgetfulness. But it can also be the verdict of a mere group which understands itself as the 'universal church', i.e. the claim of a part-church to hegemony. No part is or represents the universal whole, although it can be whole in itself. No social group represents humanity, but it does not need to be a 'split-off fragment' of humanity either. That can be helpful for understanding the local church. The local church can be whole, but not the only church, so the Latin American local churches are not a fragment of a universal church which can be understood in virtual terms. The universal church is a composite whose mandate derives from the delegation of whole local churches that are capable of life.

II. Fragmentation through colonization

In Latin America, 'fragmentation' recalls a specific colonial history. This violently interrupted and decontextualized the historical projects of the original inhabitants of America and of the African slaves who were taken away by force. The original inhabitants of America saw themselves faced for the first time in the ideology of their colonial rules with the claims of political and religious universality. 'Reduction' and 'general language' – the 'reduction' of differences and 'one language' as a form of speechlessness – were the instruments with which they operated. According to the first Jesuit provincial in the Andes, José de Acosta (1540–1600), the Babylonian confusion of more than 700 Indian languages confronted the mission with a task of bringing order which could only be coped with by a linguistic genius.[1] The Conquista and mission did not bring political and religious union to a 'fragmented' Amerindia, but fragmented its projects.[2] Therefore for formerly colonized peoples, fragmentation represents the burden following the exogenous claims of others to universality.

Fragmentation signalizes not only the destruction of memory, context and projects but also the destruction of capacities of perception. Only in situations of encounter without any socio-cultural distortion of perspectives can one get an appropriate picture of the other. For inter-cultural dialogue, asymmetry produces a diffuse dissimilarity between concepts and reality. The framework of interpretation applied by Conquistadors and missionaries to 'Latin America' often had too little to do with the reality of this continent. Nor did the concepts and ideas which the original inhabitants of America had of their 'visitors' correspond to these. Religious claims to truth can be communicated only in symmetrical conditions for communication. Thus the missionaries often confused the divine mediators of traditional religions with gods, and wrongly understood their worshippers to be polytheists. Today, by contrast, the African Cardinal Gantin claims that the traditional religions of Africa have always been strictly monotheistic.[3] But in the Afro-American religions the missionaries' saints were rapidly transformed into spirits of ancestors. If 'signs' are forced on a social group unhistorically and without a context, an uncontrollable semantic reprogramming begins. This semantic freedom can also be life-saving in apparently hopeless situations.

Colonization has exterminated peoples and destroyed cultures. But colonial interruption has not moved the survivors to culture-free areas. People never live in the longer term 'in the fragment' of destroyed cultures. It is anthropologically impossible to go back to non-cultures. Even barbarianism is not a natural condition. Social groups constantly reorganize their destroyed ways of life and use the fragments as bricks for a new whole, because they can only live in 'whole' cultures, however 'unfinished' these may be. Social misery can produce cultural ruins, but not a lack of cultural subjectivity. Colonialized Indios and enslaved Afro-Americans have constantly created projects with horizons of hope from the fragments of their cultures and those of their colonizers.

III. Religious migration

Republican freedom of religion put an end to public and legal Catholic unity. Today a large number of missionary religious groupings have their home in Latin America. The last census in Brazil, in 1991, showed that since 1980, 4,000 new religious denominations had come into being.[4] More than 30 competing Christian groupings are at present carrying on missions among the 250,000 Indios.[5] Today, all the so-called historical churches are being fragmented by Pentecostal groups which, by their words, feelings and physical form of worship, often meet very directly the need of the poor for healing, purity and another world.

Indigenous religions also participate in the process of religious migration and fragmentation. One example of this is Umbanda, which arose in 1920 in the state of Rio de Janeiro. Umbanda originally split off from Cardecistic spiritism in protest against the disqualification of Indian and African 'ancestor phenomena'. Today Umbanda is an institutionalized Brazilian religion which combines African, Indian, popular Catholic and spiritist elements. It amalgamates magical rites with a religion of redemption. African Orixas, Indian Cabolos and Catholic saints stand side by side, protect and punish on an equal footing; in some cases they are mere minions with quite imperfect human characteristics. Love of neighbour and belief in fate, dances and trances, oracles and the written word, supplement one another organically. Today this has given rise to an inter-ethnic religion of the poor and the lower middle class in the cities. An investigation carried out in connection with the last presidential election in Brazil in 1994 showed that 4.9% of those eligible to vote in Rio de Janeiro and 3.7% in São Paulo said that they belonged to Afro-Brazilian religions.[6] Umbanda is a receptacle, but also a transit camp. Of those converted to Protestant Pentecostal churches, 17% come from Umbanda and 64% from the Catholic Church. The 'grand narrative' of the 'Catholic continent' is coming to an end. But the picture of the different religious groupings with their sectors, scenarios, movements and social relevances is also becoming increasingly pluralistic internally.

The reorganization of the fragments, the freedom with which meaning is given, and the autonomy of believers from the church as an institution, make possible an almost unlimited wealth of new religious combinations.

The need for this religious migration must be seen in connection with the socio-cultural uprooting by land clearances and unemployment but also with macrocultural currents in modernity. The metropolises of Latin America have become laboratories of pluricultural encounter and ideological reorganization. Here this migration does not usually lead into the religious no man's land of secularization or atheism. Of the 4,500,000 Brazilians (4.9%) who have declared themselves to be 'religionless', only a small percentage would call themselves atheists.[7] Usually this is religious feeling without any institutional tie, i.e. a syncretism made up of fragments of different religions. Quite generally, in Latin America today one can speak of five different modes of belonging to a religion:
– a core group which is growing smaller, with firm institutional links to a religious grouping;
– a growing group of migrants from religious institutions;
– a static group which is hard to identify, belonging to two or more institutional religions;
– a group still in the minority but statistically increasing, which floats free outside the institutions;
– a very small group of 'confessing' atheists or those who are culturally secularized, with a more or less marked 'civil religion'.

IV. Counter-offensive

Fragmentariness is not just a burden resulting from modernity. It can also be the result of premodern, feudal, hierarchical structures and world-views which appeal to an other-worldly law. Finally, fragmentariness as disarticulated difference, pluralistic indifference and a proneness to myth which forgets history can also be a postmodern phenomenon.

A 'counter-offensive' concerned with the whole life of all people, and therefore with universal justice, means an understanding and shared responsibility between social groups with quite different cultural perspectives. The concerns to achieve a universality of constitutional norms for social life always presuppose efforts towards totality, identity and articulation locally. Contextuality does not mean capitulation to global structures of social inequality, but a critical counter-offensive, particularly because in connection with context and history Christians remember the incarnation of Jesus of Nazareth.

Such a counter-offensive, which seeks to respond to fragmentariness as endogenous isolation and exogenous domination, hostility or indifference, is the result of a multiplicity which shows reciprocal respect and an argumentation which imposes limits on itself. It will attempt to replace the dichotomistic 'either-or' logic with an 'and strategy' which never excludes the 'third party'. This has its difficulties, because the tares must never gain the upper hand; however, the 'pure wheat' can only be identified at harvest time. Anyone who seeks to separate the wheat from the chaff prematurely, i.e. gives a historical date to 'true' Christianity and 'universal' justice, provides a programme for violence. But anyone who relativizes the tares in such a way that they are treated like the lilies of the field is naive and becomes guilty of favouring the enemy. Reflecting on fragmentation calls for insight into the ambivalance of universality and particularity.

Even the singular voice of Latin America, with its peculiarity of language, history and society, can only be heard in the choir of macrorhetorical currents of our time which have an expiry date. Since its independence, leading elites in Latin America have wanted to construct a better Europe, and have taken part in all the scientific and ideological macrodiscourses. Positivists and evolutionists, Marxists and structuralists, functionalists and culturalists, have left behind traces of their 'grand narratives'. Since the 1920s, leading sectors of Latin America have sought their national and continental identity in the 'laboratory of races'. *The* national identity was to be produced from Indios, Africans and Europeans by mixing races. Today, finally, a policy of identity means strengthening individual socio-cultural segments of a society. Alongside 'global' liberation theology, an 'Indio theology' is taking shape. Only subjects who are not split, and whose differences are respected, can build up a whole world as articulated individuals and a social group. But traces of the elements of all the macrorhetorical discourses can be detected even in the defence of the cause of the Indios and the Afro-Americans. The autonomy of local discourse is always also crossed through with the ideology of the spirit of the age. This is true of all the literature that is produced: historiography, theology and so on. Anyone who wants to hear the pure and unbroken voice of Latin America is therefore chasing a fiction. In that case we have to criticize Octavio Paz and Euclides da Cunha, Oscar Romero and Helder Camara, after the event, for political correctness. Contextuality and the genius of a place are always fragmented by the historical expiry of dates of eras. Futhermore, they are of course also threatened by contextual blindness and particularistic striving for hegemony. So Latin America, even in the ideal case of the identity of its difference, always participates in the fragmented nature of the whole. In constructing a whole life, Latin America depends on presuppositions which it cannot guarantee by itself. Only in co-operative responsibility and solidarity can we improve the quality of our answers, which are concerned to hold together the experiment of humankind, also as a part of nature and the cosmos.

Translated by John Bowden

Notes

1. Cf. J. de Acosta, *De procuranda indorum salute*, Book One, Ch.II.5.

2. Since 1930, the Alianza Popular Revolucionária (APRA) of Peru has used the term 'Amerindia' to denote its programme of a political and cultural unity of all countries in which a majority of the population is Indian. Today Amerindia, and also Abya Yala, refers above all to an alternative project for the future linked with its autochthonous roots.

3. Cf. B. Gantin, 'Valeurs universelles des religions traditionelles africaines', *Omnis Terra* 323/35, May 1996, 198–203: 199.

4. The 1872 census showed 99.72% Catholics; in 1980 Catholics still numbered 88.9%; in 1991, approximately 80%. Source: Instituto Brasileiro de Geografia e Estatística, *Anuário Estatistico do Brasil 1994*, Rio de Janeiro 1994. For the unpublished data about religious adherence in the 1991 Brazilian census see C. James, 'Análisa de conjuntura religioso-eclesial', *Perspectiva Teológica* 28, 1996, 157–82.

5. Cf. P. Suess, 'Religiões dos povos indígenas', in Estudos da CMBB 52, *Guia para o diálogo inter-religioso*, São Paulo 1987, 67–78: 69f. For the religious pluralism in Brazil see Estudos da CNBB 62, 69, 71.

6. Cf. R. Prandi, *Raça e religião*, Novos Estudos CEBRAP 42, July 1995, 113–29: 123.

7. Ibid., 124f.

The Unity of the Church: Women's Experience

Lisa Sowle Cahill

The twentieth century has witnessed enough worldwide upheavals to make us aware as never before of the divisions and discontinuities in human history and culture: two world wars; ethnic violence and genocide broadcast globally by the mass media; the equally global reach of the nuclear threat, terrorism and environmental destruction. In the Roman Catholic Church, the expansion of the 'world church', along with the Second Vatican Council (with its positive approaches to the 'modern world' and to ecumenism), offered an umbrella of unity for the diversity of religious and cultural experience worldwide. The church seemed to promise healing for hatred and strife, calling 'the whole of humanity' and 'the whole human family' to recognize that the world is 'created and sustained by its Maker's love, fallen indeed into the bondage of sin, yet emancipated now by Christ' (*Gaudium et spes*, no. 2). But the very hope the Council engendered revealed how elusive real agreement and cooperation can be. Postconciliar controversies about 'inculturation', and about the relation between authoritative teaching and individual or local interpretation, have accentuated pluralism and fragmentation even in the church.

In the midst of this disunified, truly postmodern, ecclesial and cultural situation, women's religious experiences, forms of church engagement and theologies have erupted into view with forceful, even threatening, energy. Feminist theologians note that even the Council, in the very same paragraphs in which it addressed humanity as a whole, easily equated its audience with 'the sons of the Church', 'the world of men', and 'man's history' (*Gaudium et spes*, no. 2). The new visibility of women's experience seems, if anything, to have widened the ruptures in the unity of the church, proving that the unity for which many nostalgically yearn is an illusion.

Taken as a new 'hermeneutical key' for Scripture, church history and doctrine, the experience of women makes it clear that dominant interpretations, symbols and categories which seemed to provide past unity were constructed from a male point of view, and did not in fact include women's knowledge of and relation to God. Women's religious experience and faith have always had a vital relation to the gospel preached by Jesus and confirmed in his resurrection (of which Mary Magdalene was the first witness, according to all four evangelists). Yet women's experience has never been fully integrated into the history and self-understanding of the church, the exceptional recognition of certain more visible and influential women notwithstanding. Even the centrality of the Virgin Mary in Catholic piety has had mixed results for women. The role of the virgin mother hardly corresponds to the experience of real women, and while Mary has served as a refuge and a mediator for women and men in many cultures, Marian devotion has also encouraged women to be submissive to male authority figures and to invest all their self-worth and hope in motherhood and in sons.

Examples of androcentric biblical interpretation, religious language and imagery, doctrine, ritual, moral teaching and church law are by now familiar.[1] Among the most egregious continuing examples are the exclusive use of father and son metaphors to interpret Jesus' relationship to God, and the identification of the maleness of Jesus himself as integral and necessary to his revelation of God, God's redemption of humanity, and human beings' representation of Christ.[2] As Rosemary Ruether notes, the maleness of Jesus was a particular part of his concrete, limited, human identity, which had symbolic value in the light of his message about the inclusive love of God, especially when that message was preached in a patriarchal social setting. 'Theologically speaking, then, we might say that the maleness of Jesus has no ultimate significance . . . Jesus as the Christ, the representative of liberated humanity and the liberating Word of God, manifests . . . new humanity through a lifestyle that discards hierarchical caste privilege and speaks on behalf of the lowly.'[3] The maleness of Jesus, bringer of the reign of God, reinforces his message that male superiority is overcome and women are included as equal disciples – not that women are subordinate in God's kingdom or the church.

It has required new ways of reading Scripture and of theologizing out of women's experience to make us recognize that women and men are made equally in the image of God, and that Jesus' universal message of salvation applies equally to women and to men. Theology done on the basis of women's experience has also brought greater sensitivity to faithful women leaders in Scripture, to female images of God and Jesus in the Bible (e.g. Jesus as a mother hen in Luke 13.34), and to historical experiences of

God and Christ in female terms. Of particular interest in current theology is the symbolization of God or Jesus as the female figure of personified wisdom, Sophia (I Cor. 1.24; Luke 7.35).[4]

Yet, even though women's experience has been an important resource in the development of vital new theological currents, and of greater inclusion of both sexes in the life of the church, it is not at all clear that greater attention to women's experience is producing or should produce 'unity'. This is true for two reasons. *First*, women's experience is diverse, and the emphasis in much women's theology is *difference*, between the sexes and among cultures – not commonality. *Second*, as women's experience moves away from the false unity of a male and Eurocentric theology, it is not satisfied with mere incorporation of a few 'women's' elements into the existing androcentric model. Nor does it accept the creation of a special theological subset of 'women's issues', to which women's religious experiences and theological voices can be relegated, as if they were of interest only to women, who remain outside 'real' theology. The existing institutions of theology and church need to be radically rethought before any possibility of unity will appear on the horizon. The idea of unity itself must be radically reconceived. The future unity of a church in which women's experience is fully integrated will be a unity of constant reciprocal dialogue, of difference in community without division, but without practical or conceptual identity either.

First, women's experience and theology are pluriform. Particularity and difference are constant themes in women's theology, so much so that the very term 'feminist' is questioned by many as being too identified with a certain brand of individualist, bourgeois, white, middle-class, Western thought and activism. Even for women in European countries like France and Spain, the term 'feminism' can have connotations of separatism, antipathy toward all men, and lack of 'femininity'.[5] Speaking from her own African American experience, Toinette Eugene warns that 'the reconstructive work of feminist/womanist/mujerista reciprocity and faithful appropriation . . . can be achieved *only* through honest recognition, acceptance, and hard dialogue about difference.'[6] This point is certainly agreed upon by women from other continents, including Asia, Africa, Australia and Latin America. Kwok Pui-lan, originally from Hong Kong, says: 'Our diversity must be seen as our strength and our particularity must be cherished as the unique gift each of us can bring to the dialogical table.'[7] Yet all seek solidarity with other women cross-culturally, and most agree that women's experiences reveal areas of commonality as well as difference.

This brings us to the *second* issue of a new model of theology. Is it valid to hope for a future unity in theology and church which does include women's experience? In addition to calling attention specifically to women's experiences, and challenging androcentric interpretations of the faith, feminist theology offers a new basic understanding of theology, its methods and its aims. This understanding reflects a global, intercultural, postmodern and pluralistic approach to knowledge, although it is not relativist. Feminist theology does not aim at conceptual or practical uniformity, but at an ongoing process of mutual criticism and dialogue, in which the truth about God and human relationships is discovered inductively and experientially. The methods of feminist theology are not just intellectual and deductive; they are historical and imaginative. Its aims go beyond conceptual clarity, logical argumentation and authoritative definitions; they also include creative symbolization, evocative restatements, and heuristic proposals that stimulate insight and dialogue. Feminist theology tests truth and justice practically. 'It is not a systematically developed body of received knowledge, handed down in traditional institutions of learning. On the contrary, the emphasis is very much on "doing theology", on theology in the active mode, for it means suffering and seeking, listening and speaking, voicing and questioning, encountering and sharing, responding to and being responsible for action.'[8]

Elizabeth Johnson connects the model for feminist theology with classical theology by recalling the Augustinian insight that God is ineffable, and is best known intellectually through the negation of all symbols. In Augustine's view, God is most truly known through love. As theologians like Karl Rahner and Edward Schillebeeckx have observed, love of God includes and perhaps begins with love of other persons. A conversion to God occurs when we undergo a 'contrast experience' in which we recognize and say 'no' to the suffering of others, including women, and when we resolve to seek the flourishing of all in solidarity with one another and with God's self-offering in Christ.[9]

The feminist commitment to a dialogical and somewhat pluralistic model of truth, and to the concretization of faith in action, corresponds to some key aspects of the Catholic tradition of theology in general. Catholicism has always emphasized the communal dimension of faith. No one is saved by an individual faith act alone, but by participation in a historical, sacramental community, in which we worship and share the eucharist often. Moreover, the Catholic faith community has always been internally pluralistic, in that its basic symbols and doctrines have been subject to multiple readings. The history of theology has been a history of the dialogic reinterpretation of the Scriptures, the creeds, and the formulations of the great church councils, especially Nicaea (the doctrine of the Trinity) and Chalcedon (the doctrine of the two natures of Christ). Since the Roman Catholic Church comprises many nationalities and cultures, yet is not identified with any one, it has also been culturally pluralistic, with variety and nuance in local reappropriations of the common faith.

Moreover, as sacramental and incarnational, Catholic theology has typically emphasized the importance of life in this world, and the presence of God to humanity in and through creation and history. Thus, like feminist theology, it has put great emphasis on the importance of morality. For much of its history, Catholic moral theology has been unduly focussed on individual acts, especially sexual ones. However, it has also produced the modern papal social encyclicals, which stress the sociality and interdependence of persons, and unite the rights and responsibilities of all persons within a framework of the common good. It is precisely the full participation of women in the common good of society and the church that is the primary value and aim of feminist theology.

In conclusion, women's experience can help overcome the current fragmentation of theology and the church in two ways. It introduces a perspective and voice that had previously been excluded, repressed, or marginal, so that the content of religious symbols and theological doctrines is corrected and expanded. But more importantly, women's experience underwrites a new understanding of theology and a new model for learning and speaking theologically. Theology is not a closed system, but an ongoing process of discovery and clarification, centred on the Scriptures, common traditions of faith and practice, previous doctrinal symbols and magisterial teachings, all of which are reappropriated on the basis of the living experience of the gospel in the community of communities of believers. From the point of view of women's experience and feminist theology, the unity of the church and of theology consists in the integrity of this process, and its accountability to the presence of God in today's faith communities, as well as in traditions they inherit.

Notes

1. Among the most influential works exposing these are Mary Daly, *Beyond God the Father: Toward a Philosophy of Women's Liberation*, Boston 1973; Rosemary Radford Ruether, *Sexism and God-Talk: Toward a Feminist Theology*, Boston and London 1983; with a new introduction 1993; and Elisabeth Schüssler Fiorenza, *In Memory of Her: A Feminist Theological Reconstruction of Christian Origins*, New York and London 1983. For the expansion of women's theology and experiential critique of the Christian tradition into a variety of cultural contexts, see Ursula King (ed.), *Feminist Theology from the Third World: A Reader*, London and Maryknoll, NY 1994; and Elisabeth Schüssler Fiorenza and M. Shawn Copeland (eds.), *Feminist Theology in Different Contexts*, Concilium 1996/1. The term 'hermeneutical key' comes from the latter volume, Maria José F. Rosado Nunes, 'Women's Voices in Latin American Theology', 8.

2. Ruether, *Sexism* (n. 1), 116–38; Elizabeth A. Johnson, *She Who Is: The Mystery of God in Feminist Theological Discourse*, New York 1994, 72–3, 151–4, 163–7.

3. Ruether, *Sexism* (n. 1), 137.

4. Johnson, *She Who Is* (n. 2), 124–87; Schüssler Fiorenza, *In Memory* (n. 1), 130–40.

5. See Monika Jacobs, 'Feminist Theology in Europe', in Schüssler Fiorenza and Copeland, *Different Contexts* (n. 1), 36.

6. Toinette M. Eugene, 'How Do We Theologize Once We Recognize Difference?', in Lois K. Daly, *Feminist Theological Ethics: A Reader*, Louisville 1994, 93.

7. Kwok Pui-lan, 'Speaking from the Margins', in Daly, *Feminist Theological Ethics* (n. 6), 97.

8. King, 'Introduction', *Feminist Theology* (n. 1), 4.

9. Johnson, *She Who Is* (n. 2), 108, 62–3.

IV · Perspectives

Does the Nature of the Church Call for Unified and Clear Dogmas?

Pierre Vallin

The relationship of Christians to their history can easily lead them to imagine the doctrinal conflicts of the past as episodes in which the vocation to unity and concord in the church has been put at risk. In the accounts produced by historians or theologians these times of crisis can then have an age of reconstruction as their sequel: whatever was in danger of being scattered in fragments is remade by the inner power of the strength of yesterday and for ever, the source and principle of a doctrinal accord which is rediscovered, certain of firm and clear positions. One particularly evocative example of this logic of Christian narrative is the way in which the historical work of the Council of Trent is set in victorious opposition to the previous situation of mediaeval Western Christianities.

First of all I shall present a brief picture of these interpretations of Catholic reform. Then I shall progress to a reflection on theological presuppositions about the continuity of the Christian ecclesiastical movement and corresponding doctrinal formulations which we might prefer and promote today.

I. The work of the Council of Trent

The historians of Catholicism, especially those who pay attention to long social and cultural developments, of whom there are many in French universities, like to contrast the work of clarification achieved by the Council of Trent with the conflicts between the schools in the last three centuries of the Middle Ages. Jean Delumeau wrote in 1971: 'The Christian people needed clear and reassuring doctrine, a structured theology.' The assembly at Trent is said to have made a good response.[1] Delumeau's opinion has recently been taken up by Marc Venard, in the conclusion to his contribution to the History of the Councils published as an introduction to the edition of the Decrees of the Ecumenical Councils.[2] Another specialist, René Taveneau, in a recent study of local monastic history, says that the church of the Council of Trent 'defined its dogma' and clarified 'its relations with the secular authority'.[3]

A historical appreciation close to these but adding explicit theological connotations is given by Joseph Lecler in his 1981 conclusion to the accounts of Trent in the *Histoire des Conciles Oecuméniques*.[4] The council, this master wrote, 'by the sharpness of its definitions allowed a collective grasp of Christian faith, leaving open the possibility of deeper insights into the church'. Having written that, and doubtless thinking of Vatican I and II, Lecler adds for Trent: 'This sharpness risked becoming rigidity and inflexibility.' This last nuance gives Fr Lecler's evaluation a marked ecclesiological slant, a slant indicated by the expression 'a collective grasp of Christian faith'. Here the Catholic tradition of history writing leaves its mark.

The works of Hubert Jedin have illustrated this tradition, which can be summed up in a passage from the contribution of the great theologian to the volume edited by his colleague who continued the work in the series *Handbuch der Kirchengeschichte*.[5] As a result of the council, 'it was from the affirmation of its essence that the church drew the strength to renew itself and to maintain itself'.[6]

Although it is not strictly about doctrines but rather about the spiritual life, a statement by Joseph Lortz had already marked this perspective: 'The church was threatened with ruin; its vitality had to be revived. But this vitality is none other than the inalienable potential of holiness that the church carries within itself.'[7] Shortly afterwards, Lortz specifies that the importance of the council lies above all in the fact that 'the council was the pure incarnation of the Catholic conception of the church . . . The council presented and in part defined the church as a salvific institution, *universal, objective and founded on the papacy*.'[8] Here we see taking precise form a conception of the authority of the council which makes it the expression of a unified essence of the church, an essence present from the beginning, and still present in depth when its vitality seems extinct and doctrine is fragmented in an anarchical fashion. It has to be said that the reaffirmation by the church in council that doctrine has an organic character is not seen as sufficient of itself to prepare for a future of doctrinal accord. What is also needed is a unifying sovereign will, the visibility of the pontificate. These views reflect a decisive aspect of the ecclesiological work of the Council of Trent.

The question of the role of the papacy in relation to the Council in the first place relates to the confirmation of the decrees of Trent. This confirmation was put in writing by Pius IV in the bull *Benedictus Deus*, published at the end of June 1564, but dated January.[9] The pope feared the perversion and confusion which would arise if a Catholic, even with the best will in the world, were to produce commentaries on the acts of the council. So every explanation of this sort had to be subject to a single authority, the supreme authority of the pope. Similarly, every question which could be raised about the interpretation of the conciliar texts had to be resolved by the judgment of the Apostolic See.

The pope completed these measures with the bull *Iniuctum nobis*, which in November 1564 imposed a new formula for the profession of faith to be used by future bishops (and from now on by other faithful called to ecclesiastical office).[10] Paolo Prodi has shown that in this way Pius IV introduced a more radical change than bringing up to date the propositions contained in the profession of faith. In effect, an oath of obedience to the Roman pontiff was inserted into the Tridentine profession. Certainly oaths of obedience already existed, but in the Catholic Church the two institutions had been distinct. Now they were fused. The dogmatic profession of faith and obedience sworn by oath to the sovereign head of church form the two faces of an unprecedented institutionalization of Christian society.[11]

The oath of fidelity to the pope was expressed soberly in the profession of faith. That was no longer the case with the formulation of a complementary oath intended for future bishops. More ancient in origin, this oath was given its modern form in the *Pontificale romanum*, published under the authority of Clement VIII in 1596. An analogous formula was provided for abbots of monasteries on taking up office.[12] By this oath of obedience (the formula was to remain almost the same until 1968), the bishops bound themselves to the dispositions of the Holy See in matters of government and also swore to defend the doctrinal teachings of the Sovereign Pontiff. That completes the *Professio fidei tridentina* and develops the rule laid down by *Benedictus Deus*, which puts under the authority of the pope all the commentaries and interpretations which could be made on the decrees of the council in the future.

Paolo Prodi has shown that in this form the new Catholic institution did not have all the broadness which had been intended in the proposal presented by a number of Tridentine fathers in the spring of 1563. A faith sworn on oath was to be made obligatory for all Catholic authorities, whether ecclesiastical or civil.[13] The project was rejected when discussed; it was not to be taken up in such a broad form by the popes. By contrast, the confessional states of the Reformation often required faith to be sworn in a formula comprising two aspects: profession of faith and oath of obedience to the sovereign. However, despite this distinction, the pontifical system, too, can be defined as confessionalization. From henceforth the Roman Catholic Church was marked by a new particularity. The church was not solely to be one by the rule of the apostolic faith and the vocation of baptism, but was to form a body which had been instituted politically, its social bond constituted both by sworn adherence to a particular dogmatic systematization and by obedience to the person of the sovereign, promised under oath. While ensuring a degree of universality in the Catholic Church by contrast to the modern confessional state and nations, the Tridentine system thus consecrates in an ambiguous way the institutional fragmentation of the Christian movement.

II. The historical function of dogma: a historical analysis

The historians I have mentioned first recognize a positive function in the unification and clarification of dogma which were brought about by the Council of Trent; they say that it revived the religious coherence of Catholic populations. This evaluation is worth keeping. However, to it must be added a firm reservation based on the negative aspects of the ecclesiological change brought about by the institutional fusion between the confession of faith and an obedience sworn on oath. The role thus given to the person of the pope in maintaining the coherence of the church was in the future to be an additional obstacle in the way of interconfessional convergences or exchanges, not only *vis-à-vis* the Reformation but also in relations with the ancient churches of the East. Furthermore, did not this role put in question within the Roman Catholic Church the hope of a coherence which would be nourished by the dogmatic confession itself?

One could say that it is no coincidence, or is not just the result of human clumsiness, that the papacy has so often served to dramatize tensions among Catholics rather than being at the service of a common quest. Led to listen to the confession of faith, common research should not exclude debate nor claim to remove all uncertainties and obscurities. But this is not the kind of research which has been supported. Return at this point to a historical analysis (and the works of the authors quoted above do not contradict this), and one can think that crises like those which opposed Augustinians to Molinists, Gallicans to Ultramontanists, the liberal to the intransigent, and yet other crises of our day, owe their duration and their intensity to the action of the pontifical Curia, to its authoritarian interventions, dreaded or desired by the opposing camps, but which in both cases get in the way of a thorough debate. Similarly, the action of the Holy See has held up reflection on the modern development of science and philosophy rather than promoting serene theological reflection among Catholics.

Must these reservations of the historian about the work of the council be associated with the innovation of an oath of obedience inserted into a profession of faith? This insertion should have been denounced as theologically illegitimate. The failings which the historian will note in future Catholicism can be attributed to this deviation of a doctrinal or ecclesiological kind. But the response should be cautious, all the more so since we must always be careful about historical explanations of judgments based on theological reflections; here I agree with what Giuseppe Ruggieri has written in his study of the history of the church between theology, the humane sciences and the historical-critical method.[14]

At the same time we can think that to construct a narrative which places an event like the Council of Trent in the evolution of Christianity presupposes that one is bringing evaluations of an ethical and theological kind into play.[15] That does not necessarily happen in an explicit way; the appreciation can remain intrinsic to the narrative, and moreover can also concern events which have a less collective scope than is the case with a council. The evaluation of the ethical or anthropological issues implicit in the narratives must emerge one day or another when this is a history in which the theological options have played and play an important role. They have to appear at the level of a theological reflection which is prepared to tackle the significance of the options taken and the degree to which they are in keeping with the gospel, beyond the simple presentation, factual or doxographical, of persons and doctrines.

The innovation to which Paolo Prodi's work alerts us is evidently not susceptible to a simple ethical or theological evaluation. Anyone who is led to make indignant denunciations can be countered with a historical explanation. For example, it can be said that the way in which the role of the bishop of Rome is exercised must be adapted to circumstances; such an adaptation will have been practised in introducing the unprecedented obligation of the oath. The innovation is again explained, and justified, by analogy to what had already been introduced in several nation states which had gone over to the Protestant Reformation.

Can we, however, be content with such historical relativism which falls short of laying claim to be a critical theological evaluation? It would be a step forward to take into account the main intention of the bull *Iniuctum nobis*, the concern to make any interpretation and any commentary on the dogmatic synthesis achieved at the council subject to the authority of the Sovereign Pontiff. This aim of a doctrinal unity to be maintained at all costs instrumentalizes and in a sense relativizes the obedience owed to the pope and sworn by the bishops. But then it is in connection with this very aim that the question of an ethical and theological evaluation arises.

A classical way of bringing such an evaluation into play is presented above with the quotations from Hubert Jedin and Joseph Lortz. For them, the totalizing doctrinal work which emerged from the council corresponded to a need inscribed in the nature of the church, a nature which had pervasively been contradicted by doctrinal fragmentation. According to this type of theological evaluation, such a work of unification and clarification was the normal fruit of the vitality which naturally belongs to the church. To evaluate the work of the council according to this model corresponds to the general methodological principles of which Jedin has been the interpreter and which he has summed up like this: 'The object of the history of the church is the growth, in space and time, of the church instituted by Christ . . . It is from the science of faith that it receives this object which is his, and . . . attaches itself to it in faith.' We are in agreement that the narrative presupposes an 'object', a 'historical subject', an agent; it is the concern of Jedin's position to present this task, which we may say is that of thinking of the object church. However, does the narrative intrinsically presuppose, in the light of responsible ethical and theological evaluations, that one receives such a 'thinking of the church' from the faith? Does one have to adopt the image and concept of a society which, once instituted by its Lord, is destined to grow organically in space and time?

With this type or model of the theology of the church, the account will evaluate the work of Trent in a positive way. Here, in the logic of a growth which triumphs over temporary difficulties, will be seen the rediscovery of a unified dogmatic synthesis. The innovation which made the papacy itself a more completely sovereign and unifying church authority will be perceived as being at the service of this doctrinal unity. Fidelity to the person of the sovereign can well appear as having acquired new features, but these features are judged to have been adequately ordained for the unity of believers, according to an internal logic of growth.

Must the theologian who narrates the development of Christianity adopt such a notion of the nature or essence of his object? I do not think so. Certainly the church is given by faith, but always through and in mediations and renewals which are not truly cumulative. The image of growth in space and time is not absolutely convincing to those who have to structure a narrative of the history of the church. Similarly, completeness and clarity of dogma are not ultimate values by which one can make an evaluation.

A considered formulation of the task of the church historian has been proposed by Erwin Iserloh. His position can be summed up as follows: the account presupposes that we receive from the scriptures and the founding tradition a notion of the church, a concept which expresses the essentials in minimal form. At the same time the historian must perceive the way in which the dogmatic theologian reflects the position of such a concept. Thus Iserloh would make the church one, like Jedin, the object of the narrative which can claim to be a history of the church; but he would add that this object is not simply received by faith. It is constructed on the founding texts, and by coping with a series of theological problems. Surely the texts and reflections which are intermediaries in the process cannot be limited in such a model simply to recognizing the unity that has already been given?

Here we can introduce a polemic argument. To link the application of the Council of Trent to the generalized practice of an oath is in direct contradiction to the foundation in scripture, 'Let your yes be yes and your no, no' (Matt 5.37; James 5.12). According to Matthew, Jesus added, 'All else comes from the evil one.'

However, an ethical judgment which is led to begin there must know its limits. The condemnation which can apparently be read unequivocally out of the two sayings on oaths has been discussed and qualified by theological interpretations (the history of this has been traced by P. Prodi). However, the occurrence of this teaching in the New Testament (Matthew and James already diverge) alerts us to the ecclesiological question of the unity and clarity of doctrinal statements. The debate on the gospel ethic of the oath relates to the general diversity of scriptural affirmations, to the uncertainties about how to understand them, and to the plurality of interpretations within the prism of Christian cultures.

Taking up a view put forward by Gerhard Ebeling, I would say that the object of a narrative of the history of the church is a history of the interpretation of scripture. Without discussing the way in which this theologian understands Luther's thesis about the clarity of scripture (this article is not the place for that), we should note that this thesis makes a decisive point. The canonical text, in the very diversity of the scriptures and their obscurities, 'clearly' indicates a hoped-for, postulated coherence. Believers are called on to run the risk of condemning errors. They are to honour a rule of faith. In this light, to define the history of the church as a history of the interpretation of the scriptures is to admit that this narrative refers to an object. The narrator presupposes that his object has a coherence. This is a presupposition which can guide the reading of the doctrinal constructions to which the scriptures lead without at the same time presupposing that one can absorb the uncertainties which affect these constructions into an adequate synthesis.

In connection with the application of the Council of Trent I have suggested that a concern for unity and clarity can lead to a fragmentation which contradicts the very project of church coherence. Such a concern can get above itself, and I think that I have demonstrated an unfortunate excess of this kind. However, the possibility of excess does not mean that the quest for affirmations which are clear and harmonious must be abandoned. We are simply called on to engage in a doctrinal quest, patiently obstinate, which will not be amazed at slowness and uncertainty. The work will be solid.

Notes

1. Jean Delumeau, *Le catholicisme entre Luther et Voltaire*, Paris 1971, 43–4.
2. Marc Venard, in *Les Conciles Oecuméniques* I, Paris 1994, 335.
3. René Taveneaux, in *Bénédictines entre Saône et Meuse*, Paris 1996, 44.
4. Joseph Lecler, in *Histoire des Conciles Oecuméniques* II.1, Paris 1981, 591–2.
5. Hubert Jedin, in *Handbuch der Kirchengeschichte* 4, 1967.
6. Ibid., 533.
7. Joseph Lortz, *Histoire de l'Eglise des origines à nos jours*, Paris 1956, 222; id., *Geschichte der Kirche*, Münster[16] 1950, 82–I, 286.
8. Id., *Histoire,* 236; *Geschichte*, 301 (his italics).
9. Jedin, *Handbuch* (n. 5), 519. The complete text of the bull can be found in A. Theiner, *Acta genuina Ss. Oec. Concilii Tridentini*, Zagreb 1874, Vol. 2, 515ff.; the central part is reproduced in Denzinger-Schönmetzer, *Enchiridion*; for the parts which concern us see 1849–1850; there are extracts from the bull *Iniuctum nobis*.
10. Paolo Prodi, *Il sacramento del potere. Il giuramento politico nella storia costituzionale dell'Occidente*, Bologna 1992, 311ff.
11. Ibid., 318ff.
12. The Latin texts with French translations can be found in Victor-Daniel Boissonnet, *Dictionnaire alphabético-canonique des cérémonies et des rites sacrés* (Migne, *Encyclopédie théologique*), 1, cols. 31f. ('Abbé') and cols. 1299f. There is a summary in Pierre Dentin, *Les privileges des Papes devant l'Écriture et l'histoire*, Paris 1995, 109f.
13. Prodi, *Il sacramento* (n. 10), transcribes the text; a reference needs to be corrected: it is Vol. 9 (and not IV), 484f., of the Görres Gesellschaft series *Concilium Tridentinum*.
14. In the composite work *Église et histoire de l'Église en Afrique*, Paris 1990, 347–63.
15. Cf. my 'Discours théologique et pratique historiennes' in the composite study *Histoire et Théologie*, Paris 1994, 33–57, which contains references to the authors (Jedin, Iserloh, Ebeling) who will be cited.

The Unity of the Believer in Question

Jean-Pierre Jossua

A loss of unity

Christian experience has been marked in the past by a strong internal unity coming from outside the subject, at least in the way in which individuals could represent themselves. There was an entire integration, of which I shall emphasize three major aspects.

In the West, from the Middle Ages, individuals belonged to a church which was one, despite its institutional crises; and the break which came at the Reformation – even if it deeply shook more people than might appear – finally issued in partial unities which claimed to be universal: everyone is supposed to believe and live in the same way, and thus individuals are not divided within their religious beliefs. Secondly, these religious beliefs left their stamp on culture, and human thought was as it were included within the theological architecture. What intellectual elaboration did not really succeed in achieving, ecclesiastical control imposed in authoritarian fashion. Thus the unity of the thinking and believing subject in principle remained assured. Finally, the unity between Christian convictions and the church as a specific gathering on the one hand and civil society on the other – in the form of the symbiosis that was called Christendom – supposedly ensured that individuals experienced a unity between their human tasks and their faith, between their social life and their membership of the church.

This is not the place to describe how this unity has progressively broken up between the sixteenth century and our own, with a pluralism which was first religious and then in part non-religious. This modified the very position of faith, along with the secularization of society and culture (science, history, philosophy, art, politics, morality and so on). It happened despite the construction of an almost totalitarian ideology and an institutional form of functioning in the church, of a defensive sub-culture, and of a plan to reconquer society which was first political and then cultural. Outside very narrow circles and despite recent attempts at restoration on the part of neo-conservative movements, this internalized external framework no longer seems to be operative.

A re-creation of unity

The creative reaction of the conscience and the gospel community has been a strong subjectification of unity, overcoming the forces of fragmentation which are at work in the modern world without denying them. To give as meaningful an account as possible, I shall describe the 'confessing' form of this re-creation among Catholics (which moreover is close to the Protestant forms which preceded it), leaving aside the 'liberal' mixtures. And since my task is limited to the Christian experience – as distinct from the confession of faith – I shall describe briefly some aspects of this experience which to a certain degree correspond to the elements in the external unity evoked above. I shall not return to the unity of thought, since that would take me outside the topic which has been assigned to me. This recapture of a style of existential unity in the Christian subject is so striking, in the face of what now seems to be an insurmountable division in the human being, that it has been able to be a major factor arising from commitment to the gospel and verification of the meaning and reality of faith.

In affirming that the experiences that I referred to were those of everyone, I left it until this point to describe a second element. These experiences are felt to be common to several people, and not strictly particular. They are also common in a more original sense, in that the Christian experience is collective, social and historical before being appropriated by individuals. This element implies services of unity, a transmission in time and space of the elements which comprise the foundation of Christianity; so this is once again an institutional element. However, it must also be said that here, as always, from now on the priority lies with the basic communities and interpersonal networks (which have more of a real communal value than is attributed to them); it is on the unity which they live out and the gift of the Spirit which brings them into being that one counts first and foremost, without minimizing the need for ministries of communion. And that allows us to understand how this new – yet very old – form of unity is radically ecumenical, on the basis of what is essential (with the 'hierarchy of truths' which is a correlate of it) and of the acceptance of differences (which are conceived of as riches, not as obstacles).

I think that where unity is concerned, everything to which I have just referred is experienced at its deepest level in different forms – more or less pure and more or less conscious – by the liveliest Christianity of the twentieth century. However, a third element must be added which is no less important. Faith does not simply bind together what is specific and, if one wills, religious, in the bundle of Christian experience. It offers a form of original unity to the whole of existence, in its full respect for human intermediaries and therefore for the 'secularization' – an absence of any direct and normative religious reference – of all sectors of culture. (I have already mentioned the effect of this.) Under the sign of faith in the one God, Creator and Saviour, and the spiritual offering of existence (Rom. 12.1), a superior unity can be experienced which is sometimes represented by setting the gospel against human realities (politics, ethics) without denying the autonomy of a pluralist quest. Sometimes this will go hand in hand with a more emphatic neutrality (science, 'human sciences'), but it will always reject a deductive attitude, a telescoping of intermediaries in the name of a superior truth or an authoritarian resolution of new or simply open questions. There is no point in dwelling at length on the fact that this is the source of the profound institutional malaise (criticism, detachment, practical indifference) of present-day Catholics over the authorities of their church.

New upheavals

If that is the new experience of existential unity which several generations of confessing Christians, committed to the church, have been led to live out, we must now take stock of unprecedented situations which can be recognized around us, experiences of the fragmentation of the Christian being which go much farther. They take this form of a unity that is opposed to itself, leading to doubts about its transmission, and even to destabilization. Do we in fact have to think that these upheavals represent the radicalization of certain features of this unity, and thus that they lead to suspicion about its consistency?

In the 1960s, particularly among Christians who had been led to set their faith alongside the 'human sciences' and to carry on an inner dialogue between the two, we can discover the internalization of a stable element of 'unbelief' or an alternation between 'faith' and 'doubt'. This was something quite different from the rhetoric of 'the unbelief of believers' (dramatizing the structural part of the lack of evidence in faith or the 'bad faith' of believers over certain supposed 'dogmas'). And we may be disconcerted at this. Our friends told us sincerely that they were part believers and part not, sometimes one and sometimes the other. In fact this attitude could not but remind us that we, too, gave intellectual uncertainty a place in our faith. However, the decisive difference was that in us 'yes' had the final say in the discussion; there was a certainty of commitment and thus an ultimate unity in the believing subject. Now this instability seems to be accepted by many people as self-evident.

More recently, one has been able to observe a new religious position among young adults and even more among those younger still: a kind of partial and spasmodic Christianity, very different from the whole and permanent commitment which was ours. A partial Christianity: they hold to this and not to that, calmly, without scruples and without challenging the institution. Sometimes they even add heterogeneous elements acquired in the world supermarket of religions, snatched from other coherent ensembles, tinkered around with and introduced in an incoherent way into the religious whole which emerged from the Bible (metempsychosis, for example). To keep to the partial character, it has to be recognized that our own way of making critical choices in the church tradition or in the elements which the church authorities tended to impose were by no means dissimilar. However, these choices were justified hermeneutically – rightly or wrongly – and made on the basis of the 'hierarchy' evoked above: 'original sin', 'hell', 'infallibility' do not have the same central position as the 'divinity' of Christ or 'eternal life'. The recentring even had the affect of increasing commitment and above all unity.

Theirs is also a spasmodic Christianity. This is true of the times when they join in with the Christian community, which are occasional, indeed rare. The places are eclectic and many. And here there is a total innocence and irresponsibility. Here again, our rejection of legal regulations – those that lie between what the obligatory and the forbidden – about what is essentially free and festive, and our rejection of the imprisonment of what is in part Christian invention in a compulsory ecclesiastical framework, can be compared to these more recent developments. But one of our essential preoccupations has been the integral nature of Christian experience with its different elements, as the fruit of its faithfulness and the condition of its fertility. Another preoccupation has been responsibility for the church, despite the wear caused by vain combats on opposed fronts, fought for a balance between transmission and innovation.

Now if we find these attitudes disconcerting, it is because they do not necessarily stem from the disaffection which almost ended up in disengagement from 'practice' which was thought obligatory, or in 'liberal' withdrawal into a minimal ('rational' or 'humanist') interpretation of the faith. In fact they seem to arise less from a disinvestment than from cultural situations which affect all forms of belonging and adherence; they would only seem possible to a certain degree and for a certain time. One could speak of a pathology of choice: of indecision, of stability, of zapping. The fact is there, connected with a development in the relationship to time, to social stability (local, professional, conjugal, and so on), to the putting of all ideas in question, and to the offer of all things to those who can acquire them. And it is hard to see how this could change soon. At the same time one can understand that these uncertain, partial and spasmodic commitments beyond question represent the *maximum commitment possible*, and not indifference; one can be convinced that it is indispensable to welcome them if one wants there to be believers tomorrow.

However, a belonging which is so relative and, once again, an experience which is shaken, are faced with formidable problems – since its acceptance presupposes something permanent and global in others. Can Christian faith exist and be credible without unity, interiorized from outside or developed existentially, which has always been one of its essential attributes?

The Pilgrim State of the Christian Church

Gregory Baum

A Search for a Pastoral Ecclesiology

We are in need of a pastorally-sensitive ecclesiology that interprets for Christians their actual experience of the church: their faithful attachment to the gospel and the Christian tradition, their confusion over the disunity of the Christian church, and their anguish over many aspects of ecclesiastical life and teaching that appal them.

The ecclesiology of Vatican II tried to overcome the institutional understanding of the church as *societas perfecta* by emphasizing its spiritual or mysterious character. The church is created by the gifts of God: Christ present in Word and Sacrament, and the Spirit uniting the faithful in a single communion. Here is a sentence from the Decree on Ecumenism: 'The Holy Spirit dwelling in the faithful and pervading and and ruling the entire Church brings about that marvellous communion among the faithful that joins them so intimately in Christ, making him the principle of the Church's unity.'[1] Yet is this 'marvellous communion' confirmed by the experience of Christians?

Vatican II also left us confused in regard to the status of the Catholic Church as the one true church of Christ. While the Decree on Ecumenism acknowledges the means of grace and the life of grace in the other churches and honours their role in the economy of salvation, it continues to affirm the Catholic Church as the one church in which the fullness of truth and grace prevails. Yet the decree does not explain what this means. In fact it uses the term 'fullness' in two almost contradictory senses: it speaks of the fullness of truth, grace and the means of salvation presently available in the Catholic church,[2] and at the same time of the fullness with which Christ wants his earthly body to be endowed, which fullness lies in the future and represents the aim of the ecumenical movement.[3] But if fullness is a

Spirit-guided task to be achieved in future history, how can any church claim this fullness at the present time?

In 1877 John Henry Newman, later to become a cardinal, dared to propose a pastorally-sensitive ecclesiology in the preface to the third edition of his *Via Media*, a collection of essays published decades earlier when he was still an Anglican.[4] Now writing his preface as a Catholic, Newman offered the following ecclesiological reflection. He recognized three offices rightfully exercised by the church: the prophetic, the priestly and the royal. These offices, assigned by divine appointment, were to interact and support one another. The prophetic office assured the rule of truth, but left to itself it was tempted by rationalism; the priestly office drew the faithful into prayer and worship of God, but left to itself it was tempted by superstition; the royal office led the faithful to sanctity by rules and regulations, but left to itself it was tempted by ambition and tyranny. The church corresponded to the divine intention when these three offices interacted and rescued one another from their temptations. Worship would temper rationalism, truth would overcome superstition, and piety would soften the ruling hand.

Newman's ecclesiology enabled Catholics to interpret their experience of the church. It explained to them what happened when they suffered under a magisterium that knew too much, when they were introduced to devotions that made them uncomfortable, and when they were led by popes and bishops that acted like feudal lords. But Newman's ecclesiology also explained why, despite the distortions, Christians continued to love the church: they recognized the church's divinely-granted powers to summon forth a holy community.

Newman's intuition that ecclesiology must attend to the church's threefold ministry in its sociological reality deserves recognition. Since the days of Newman, the development of a sociology of religion has introduced many ideas that help theologians to arrive at a better understanding of the earthly, Spirit-possessed reality of Christ's church.

The mediocrity of organized religion

Thoughtful sociologists have recognized that organized religion on a large scale is a social reality that is intrinsically conflictual. In a famous work[5] Ernst Troeltsch has shown that large churches, as contrasted with small sects, are organizations subject to many tensions created by the needs to please the worldly rulers, adjust to the society in which they exist, and take into account the various religious trends existing within them. Churches must compromise. A widely-cited article by Thomas O'Day has analysed what he called the five dilemmas of the institutionalization of religion.[6]

The article shows that large-scale, organized religion, including the Christian church, can survive and thrive only through a series of compromises.

Let me mention, using my own terminology, the dilemmas described by O'Day and explored by other sociologists. In all organizations, including the church, there exists a tension between the logic of mission and the logic of management.[7] The logic of mission calls for fidelity to the purpose which the organization was created to serve, while the logic of management demands the protection of the means that allow the organization to survive and grow. Both logics exercise an important role. Yet what happens in all institutions, including the churches, is that only too often the decision-makers at the top assign priority to the logic of management. To assure the church's privileged status and economic viability, ecclesiastical leaders often prefer to remain in solidarity with the rich and powerful and turn a deaf ear to the biblical message demanding social justice and solidarity with the poor. Yet even with the best will in the world, abstracting from sin, the conflict between the two logics is inescapable. Why? Because an organization can exercise its mission only if the needs of the institution, modest as they may be, are adequately met. Some compromise becomes necessary.

Related to the first dilemma is a second, between coercion and persuasion. How is order to be kept in the organization? Should the ecclesiastical government use coercion to make its members conform to the common norm, or should it protect the truth with sound arguments as the only weapon? Here again, the dilemma is inescapable: for both forms of governance are necessary. There are situations when even the most gentle ecclesiastical leaders will draw a line and excommunicate the dissident party – for instance, two decades ago the World Alliance of Reformed and Presbyterian Churches excommunicated the Afrikaner Church, unwilling at that time to repudiate apartheid.

Other unresolvable dilemmas exist between adaptation to new social and cultural conditions and conservative attachment to the old ways, between the objectification of faith in doctrine and ritual and the existentialist quest for the personal meaning of faith, and between the centralization of church life and the freedom exercised by local communities. To these five dilemmas others could be added.

The point I wish to make is that these dilemmas cannot be resolved in permanent fashion: they keep on creating tension, conflicts, disappointments and frustrations. Organized religion can thrive only through a series of successful compromises. The larger the ecclesiastical body, the greater the tensions and the greater the need for mediating positions acceptable to the members for the sake of social peace, even if these positions do not quite correspond to their deepest convictions. There is something inevitably mediocre about large-scale organized religion. This is the pilgrim state of the early church, which Vatican II has acknowledged but the meaning of which it has not explored.

The preceding analysis, you will note, has bracketed the reality of sin in the church. Once the selfish quest for power and privilege is taken into account, as for instance in Newman's ecclesiology, the internal tensions become even greater. What is called for in this situation goes far beyond the wisdom of compromise between legitimate aspirations: what is now demanded is conversion, i.e. renewed fidelity to the gospel. According to the Decree on Ecumenism, 'Christ summons the Church, as she goes her pilgrim way, to that continual reformation of which she always has need, insofar as she is an institution of humans here on earth. Therefore, if the influence of events or of the times has led to deficiencies in conduct, church discipline or even the formulation of doctrine . . . these should be appropriately rectified at the proper moment.'[8]

The proper moment is often delayed. There are many Christians today who are moved by the life and teaching of Jesus Christ and desire to embody the gospel in their lives and their social commitments, yet who look upon the church simply as a necessary evil, necessary because they construct their networks of cooperation within the church, yet evil because of its institutional self-absorption. Yet such a utilitarian ecclesiology is theologically inadequate. One reason for this is that the gospel, i.e. the message of Jesus and his life, death and resurrection, has been handed on to us by the Christian tradition, including the Scriptures, and if this tradition were not inhabited by the Spirit, we could not rely on what we have received from it.

Una, sancta, catholica et apostolica

In Newman's down-to-earth ecclesiology the role of the Word and the Spirit in the church is a dynamic one, the summoning forth of a balanced interaction among its diverse ministries, rescuing them from their intrinsic temptations. In more general terms, the Word communicates the Spirit to the church and the Spirit teaches the church to listen to the Word. If we assume this interdynamic role, what does it mean to proclaim the church as *una, sancta, catholica et apostolica*? The following remarks offer a few hints: they intend to show that even in the pilgrim state of the church inevitably marked by mediocrity, the Spirit is at work performing *mirabilia Dei*.

The church is 'apostolic' in its Spirit-inspired efforts to be faithful to the gospel and interpret it as the good news for the society in which it lives.

This takes place through the cooperation of many. The effort involves personal conversion, the rereading of scripture and tradition, the intervention of local communities, exegetical and theological studies, the guidance of church authorities, and the birth of prophetic movements. The church is 'catholic' in its Spirit-inspired efforts to incarnate the gospel without violence in many different cultures and transcend within itself the discriminations and structured inequalities created by the sinful world. A church that does not recognize the equality of men and women in its ministry damages its catholicity. The church is 'holy' in its Spirit-inspired efforts to become a community of disciples. These efforts include the recognition of the gratuity of divine grace, the openness to God in prayer and public worship, the solidarity with the poor and the weak, and the commitment to a life of love, justice and peace. The church is 'one' in its Spirit-inspired efforts to appreciate anew the unifying gifts it has received, including message, sacraments and ministry, and to promote an ecumenical movement that seeks to overcome the divisions in Christ's earthly body. 'Concern for restoring unity pertains to the whole Church, laity and clergy alike. It extends to everyone, according to the potential of each, whether it is exercised in daily Christian living or in theological and historical studies. This very concern already reveals to some extent the bond of solidarity existing among all Christians, and it leads toward the full and perfect unity which is God's loving desire.'[9]

This is how one conciliar text describes the dynamic presence of the Spirit in the church. 'The People of God believes that it is led by the Spirit of the Lord, who fills the earth. Motivated by his faith, the people labours to decipher authentic signs of God's presence and purpose in the happenings, needs and desires in which it has a part along with other men (and women) of the age. For faith throws a new light on everything, manifests God's design for humanity's total vocation, and thus directs the mind to solutions that are fully human.'[10]

Notes

1. *Unitatis redintegratio*, 2.
2. Ibid., 3.
3. Ibid., 24.
4. See John Henry Newman, *Via Media*, Preface to the third edition, par. 2, 4. In the most recent English edition, John Henry Newman, *The Via Media of the Anglican Church*, Oxford 1990, see 25–6.
5. Ernst Troeltsch, *Die Soziallehren der christlichen Kirchen und Gruppen*, first published in 1911: English translation, *The Social Teaching of the Christian Churches* (1931), reissued New York 1960.
6. Thomas O'Day, *The Sociology of Religion*, Englewood Cliffs, NJ 1966, 90–7.

7. For the development of this distinction, see Gregory Baum, *Theology and Society*, New York 1987, 230–46.

8. *Unitatis redintegratio*, 6.

9. Ibid., 5.

10. *Gaudium et spes*, 11.

Fragments and Forms: Universality and Particularity Today

David Tracy

I. Introduction: catholicity, particularity, universality

When any appeal to 'universality' conceals uniformity, particularity may be honoured in name but not in fact. Many modern systems of thought (including Cartesianism, Hegelianism and officially sanctioned neo-Scholasticisms) were totality-systems that disallowed genuine particularity. The church Catholic, at its best, has always honoured true catholicity. The church Catholic always knew that real catholicity is always in danger. Catholicity is diversity-in-unity. False catholicity, on the other hand, is just as frequent in ecclesial history: it is an appeal to any form of universality that uneasily masks a totality-system designed to render all particularities either finally harmless and insignificant or significant and therefore harmful.

The issue of particularity and universality can be reformulated, therefore, as follows: is it or is it not the case that, however particular in origin and expression any classic work of art or any tradition of specialities may be, the effects of its classics can be, in principle, universal? To shift the questions of particularity and universality away from origins to effects is a first step. My own work on the nature of all particular classics has led me to this conclusion. To summarize: every classic work of art or religion is highly particular in both origin and expression, yet can be universal in effect. Dante, the Florentine, knew this well as he produced his universal classic, *The Divine Comedy*. Indeed, Dante, in his Christian in-carnational-poetic imagination, always knew that the universal was formed in the particular (Beatrice), not outside it. The Christian imagination is always open in and through the particular Jesus who is the Christ (finds universality). Then the Christian finds that other particularities (again Beatrice) are grounded in and transformed by the concrete universal, the

Form of forms, Jesus the Christ. As reception-theory in modern hermeneutics attempts to show that, even if we cannot agree on the *origins* of a classic work of art, we can still agree on its effects. Those effects can only be described as public and, in the greatest classics, universal, i.e., shareable, open to all human beings. The effects of any classic work of art or the classic symbols and narratives, rituals of particular spiritual and theological traditions, can become universal by hermeneutically providing disclosive and transformative possibilities for all reflective persons. Their universality, indeed their meaning and truth, is their ability to disclose new transformative possibilities for the imagination of any inquirer. The spectrum of possible responses (as disclosive and transformative) to any classic varies widely, ranging from a tentative sense of resonance on the one end of the spectrum, to the other end, where the experience is more appropriately described as a 'shock of recognition'. In *every* case along the whole spectrum, however, *some* hermeneutical disclosure – transformation and thereby some meaning and truth – is, in fact, present, and present as communicable, shareable, universal, catholic.

If strictly positivist and instrumentalist notions of universality as uniformity and univocity are alone allowed, then the possibility of the common concrete experience of the truths of art and spirituality as truth-as-disclosure and transformation in and through the particular is, of course, disallowed. Then, as the very concept of universality becomes more and more scientized and technicized, art becomes marginalized and religion privatized. But if – to employ classic Aristotelian terms – poetics and rhetoric are also allowed to make claims to universality (poetics through the disclosure-transformation in particular works), the range of universality itself is properly expanded – and properly focused in the *de facto* effects of particular works. Theologically construed, this hermeneutical insight yields the model of catholicity as diversity-in-unity, universality through concrete particularity. We need to shift the discussion of universality and particularity away from origins to effects. In that shift, the role of any classic tradition of spirituality of theology or any new candidate for classical status lies in the new religious, spiritual and theological movements (e.g. the new theologies from Asia, Africa, Latin America and the formerly silenced theologies of Europe and North America, such as the new African-American, native American and Hispanic theologies of North America).

It is not the case, therefore, that our only alternatives are a positivist and instrumentalist definition of the public universality as univocity and uniformity or a sheer chaos, a multiplicity of positions on theological meaning, and truth.

Any classic tradition, after all, is always particular and yet can become universal as a phenomenon whose excess and permanence of meaning resists definitive interpretation. The classics of art, as well as classic religious, spiritual and theological movements, are phenomena whose truth-value is dependent upon their disclosive and transformative possibilities for the interpreters. The concrete classics of art and religion are likely to manifest disclosive and transformative meaning and truth in a manner that is not reducible to uniformity. Catholic truth is always diverse. Truth as a disclosure-transformation of universality in and through particularity (Heidegger, Gadamer, Ricoeur) is available in principle to all who will risk entering into genuine conversation with the classic spiritual and theological movements of our plural, Catholic traditions.

The classics appear with a claim to disclosure, a claim to attention as *ours* – i.e. as those willing to enter into conversation with them. As conversation-*partners* we must remain open to the risk of a retrieval of their disclosures. As *conversation*-partners, we must remain equally open to any necessary critique or suspicion of the errors and systematic distortions also possibly present in our classic traditions and in the history of their effects. Every great work of civilization, as Walter Benjamin justly observed, is also a work of barbarism. Every great classic, every classic tradition, including every classic spiritual tradition, needs both retrieval and critique-suspicion. Every classic needs continuing conversation by the community constituted by its history of effects. When that community is both Catholic and catholic, universality will be acknowledged as genuine diversity-in-holistic unity.

II. Particularities as fragments

The real face of our period, as Emmanuel Levinas saw with such clarity, is the face of the other: the face that commands 'Do not kill me'. The face insists: do not reduce me or anyone else to your narrative. Each of us, for example, can accept evolutionary theory for understanding nature as well as understanding ourselves as part of nature. But natural evolutionary theory is not useful for understanding myself as a subject active in history. There I, like you, am other and different. No one should be viewed as simply more of the same, merely a moment in the grand social evolutionary teleological schema of modernity. Genuine thought today begins in ethical resistance; it begins by trying to think the unthought of modernity. Beyond the early modern turn to the purely autonomous, self-grounding subject, lies the quintessential turn of much contemporary thought – the turn to the other. It is that turn which principally defines the intellectual as well as the ethical meaning of our peculiar moment.

The other and the different come forward now as central intellectual categories across all the major disciplines, including theology. The others and the different – both those from other cultures and those others not accounted for by the grand narratives of the dominant culture – return with full ethical force to unmask the secretly social evolutionary narrative of modernity as ultimately an implausible reading of our human history together.

God's shattering otherness, the neighbour's irreducible otherness, the othering reality of 'revelation', not the consoling modern notion of 'religion': all these expressions of genuine otherness demand the serious attention of all thoughtful persons, especially those in search of Catholic unity-in-diversity.

As we recover the 'otherness' and difference in the 'subjugated know-ledges' (Foucault) of our complex and pluralistic Catholic heritage, we also have the great opportunity to learn from the new 'other' forms of theology and spirituality, philosophy and culture flourishing throughout the Catholic world. Sometimes the best we can hope for today is the recovery of some intellectual and spiritual 'fragments' of our own and other traditions.

But note the shift in sensibility in appeals to the familiar contemporary metaphor of 'fragments' to describe our situation. A neo-conservative thinker like T. S. Eliot will appeal to the image of 'fragments' as all we have left 'to shore up against our ruin', as Eliot moved poetically from the contemporary *Wasteland* to the moving, fragmentary Christian theolog-ical resources of *Ash Wednesday* and the *Four Quartets*. A far more positive approach to fragments is also possible, however: recall how Walter Benjamin, that brilliant dialectical revisionary Marxist oddly and uneasily united to a kind of revisionist kabbalist, also appealed to the metaphor of 'fragments' with very different resources and readings from those of any neo-conservative: the fragments of life embedded in kabbalistic readings of Messianic Judaism or Franz Kafka's readings of fragmented modern life gave hope, not resignation, to Benjamin's thought. So, too, the fragments of biblical apocalyptic and lamentations traditions disclose hope to several Jewish and Christian thinkers today. Finally, consider a third use of the metaphor 'fragments'. Many post-modern thinkers from Bataille to Kristeva also appeal to the metaphor of 'fragments': now as expressions of excess and transgression which may free us, however transiently, from the asphalt highway of modern rationality and traditionalist uniformity. Indeed for many post-moderns only the fragmentary and marginalized resources in our history – the avant-gardes, the mad, the hysterics, the mystics – will help us finally to glimpse the emancipatory phenomena of 'otherness' and 'difference' in subjugated counter-traditions to modernity and thereby free us from 'more of the same' (Foucault).

These three distinct – even conflicting – appeals to 'fragments' show us new fragments in new cultural situations. What we now possess most clearly are fragments of our heritage and new fragments from new cultural situations. And through these highly particular fragments we find hope for a true catholicity as unity-in-diversity. Surely we need a genuinely new vision of reasonable hope. Since the Enlightenment, modern thought has defined itself in terms of too hardened a set of once-flexible categories. This misreading has been intensified in our period by the sometimes stridently defensive moves of the proponents of modernity and the equally strident outcries of many anti-moderns and post-moderns. We may need to step back for a moment and examine, as calmly and deliberately as we can, the origins, the rich, flexible passage our church is taking as it moves from a Eurocentric to a world church. Then our fragments – pre-modern, modern and post-modern – may not simply shore us up against our ruin, nor merely help us undo the totality – thinking and totalitarian and colonizing temptations of false versions of catholicity. Instead we may find ourselves with another kind of hope altogether: more modest, more willing to admit our present polycentric Catholic situation, more honest in insisting that fragments are our best possession and that all the Catholic forms – all the pre-modern, modern and contemporary fragments – are our best hope for creating a new unity-in-diversity worthy of both the pluralistic Great Tradition and the polycentric ecclesial and cultural post-Eurocentric present.

III. Fragment and forms: the hope of unity-in-diversity

The central ideal of Western thought from its beginning in Greece (or even, before classical Greece, as argued by Mircea Eliade in his studies of archaic religious manifestations) was the idea of the real as, in essence, its appearance in form. For the ancients, the essence of the real and our knowledge of it consists ultimately of form. Form, moreover, shows forth the real in harmonious appearance: whether in sensuous image as in Greek sculpture; in mathematics as in Pythagoras; in forms of tragedy which render some aesthetic harmony even to chaos and strife; above all, through the ancient philosophical turn to reflective form in the soul or mind. For the ancients the essence of the real and our knowledge of it consists ultimately of form. The real appears in an orderly way and thus becomes (even in tragedy) harmonious appearance. This aesthetic, i.e. form-focussed, understanding of the real provided the ultimate grounding for any harmonious synthesis of the cosmic, the divine and the human realms among the ancients. It is a difficult thought to comprehend for us late twentieth-century heirs of the fragmentation of all syntheses. It is even more difficult for us as inheritors of a hermeneutics of suspicion that every form may merely mask indeterminacy and every appearance or manifestation may always already hide a strife involving both disclosure and concealment.

Nevertheless, both critics and proponents of classical, mediaeval and much modern thought (Bruno to Hegel) cannot grasp Western thought without dwelling on the centrality of form. For the pre-moderns, what appears or manifests itself through form is not our subjective construction but the very showing forth, through form, of the real. For the Greeks real being begins with intelligible form, i.e. with a multiplicity, chaos, strife rendered somehow orderly and harmonious through form. The Jewish and Christian thinkers accepted the centrality of form but could not accept the necessity of form in Greek and Roman thought. The Greek gods need the form principle; indeed the form is divine and the divine is form for the Greeks. For the Jew, Christian and Muslim, God creates form. But as long as God is not understood as exclusively a purely transcendent will and as long as God's actions are not read exclusively through efficient causality, form survives, indeed prevails: now through the Creator-God's formal, immanent causality. For Christian thought, moreover, the doctrine of the Word grounded this reality of form in the central Christian doctrines of christology and Trinity.

This principle of reality manifested *as real* in and through harmonious form in-form-ed the Western philosophical ontotheological tradition from Plato to Hegel. For Plato, with all his constant rethinking of 'form', especially in *Parmenides*, form in some manner resided within the appearing objects of which it constituted the intelligible essence. As the determining factor of that intelligibility (and thereby reality) form also surpassed the objects. In Greek philosophy (including Aristotle, despite his critique of Plato on form) being is defined in terms of form. Moreover, form's dependence is to be understood primarily, not exclusively, in terms of participation. The same is also true, it might be added, of archaic and Greek religion as manifestation (Eliade) or, as Hegel nicely named Greek religion, the religion of beauty. The same centrality of form, as Balthasar shows, is true of any form of Christianity faithful to the incarnational principle and to a properly theological understanding of Word as Logos, i.e. manifestation in and through form. Moreover, for Hegel, all content attains its truth in and through form.

The ancients, moreover, held that truth does mean 'to be justified' (as for the moderns), but that justification can be found principally in the sense that truth means participation in being (not construction of it) as manifested through particular forms. This ancient sense is also the one argued by modern hermeneutics: first, by Hans-Georg Gadamer in his insistence in *Truth and Method* that truth is fundamentally disclosure, and is best rendered through form (*Dar-stellung*, not *Vor-stellung*); second, and most carefully, by Paul Ricoeur in his contemporary argument that truth is primordially manifestation, and only derivatively correspondence or even coherence, allied to Ricoeur's further hermeneutical question of how the world of possibility of the manifestation is rendered through the forms of composition, genre and style. Any theologian who argues, on contemporary grounds, in favour of a hermeneutical understanding of truth as primordially manifestation through some particular form cannot but be heartened by new explosions of different forms (narrative, ritual, symbol, concept) in contemporary theologies.

Particularities in our period may well have yielded to fragments. But those fragments are the new forms that disclose the hope of every move beyond both mere fragmentation and a literally hope-less uniformity: the hope of encouraging universality through concrete forms (Section I); unity-in-diversity through difference and otherness both now viewed as fragments of a Catholic whole (Section II); now forms from all the new theologies and new spiritual movements so alive in our contemporary church (Section III). Catholicity is such universality in and through the diverse particular, fragmentary forms of the whole church and whole tradition.

In our own period, moreover, many particular Catholic traditions-of-theology, spirituality, philosophy, art are willing to acknowledge their fragmentation from former dreams to encompass the whole of Catholic reality (for its real unity amidst ever-increasing particular diversity). The best of the new theologies and spiritualities, as well as the philosophies and works of art from the emerging world church, acknowledge both their partial character (as parts of the greater Catholic unity in diversity) and their strong role as new fragmented forms (indeed, old and new fragments and old and new forms) empowered to unmask any totality system attempting, yet again, to honour particularity merely nominally while in fact it levels all otherness, difference, diversity.

'Kill them all; God will know God's own' was not merely a notorious saying in the midst of the campaign against the mediaeval Cathari. Unfortunately for our ambiguous history, the Cathari are not the only noble, brilliant, fragmentary cultural and spiritual movement that has been levelled by the reigning totality system of the period under the banner of universality as uniformity. Perhaps in our own day where 'otherness' and 'difference' (not merely particularity) have become so prominent, there is a new opportunity for all to affirm as both catholic and Catholic the new and old forms and fragments of the Great Tradition as it expands exponentially in our period past its Eurocentric origins into a world church, filled again with vibrant new forms, particularities, differences, into a new Catholic and catholic unity-in-diversity.

Bibliography

1. On hermeneutics:
Hans-George Gadamer, *Truth and Method*, London ²1981
Paul Ricoeur, *Le conflit des interprétations*, Paris 1969
Paul Ricoeur, *Interpretation Theory*, Fort Worth 1976

2. On form:
Louis Dupré, *The Passage to Modernity*, New Haven 1985

3. On religious classics:
David Tracy, *The Analogical Imagination: Christian Theology and the Culture of Pluralism*, New York and London 1980.

Towards What Unity of the Churches?

Johannes Brosseder

I. Theological and ecclesiological foundations

In his lecture on Psalm 45 from the year 1532 Martin Luther observes:

> The church is not holy and pure in itself, but it is holy in its head Christ, and it is pure in the name of Christ . . . The church must therefore be recognized and believed in as holy. However, it cannot be seen as such; as the Creed says, 'I believe in one holy church', and not 'I see one holy church.' If you want to judge by what you see, you will see it as a sinner; you will see frail brethren (as they say); you will see one give offence through lack of feeling and immoderation, another give offence through his anger, and yet another give offence in some other way. Therefore it is not written 'I see', but 'I believe in' one holy church, because it has no righteousness of its own. But this righteousness comes from Christ who is its head, and in this faith I perceive its holiness . . .[1]

What Luther says here about the holiness of the church with reference to the creed of the early church similarly applies to its unity. This word opens up a theological horizon which must not be distorted by reflection on the question towards what unity the Christian churches are or should be moving. In effect this horizon of the baptismal creed and confession of faith of the early church means: 'I believe in the Holy Spirit, and in this faith I believe in the one, holy catholic and apostolic church as a work of the Holy Spirit.' In this faith the present-day Christian churches, all of which stand by this creed, confess the one church as the work of the Holy Spirit: regardless of the breaking and establishment of church communion by the churches it is 'given' and 'exists' as before. This unity has not been made a 'state' and an 'essence' by the church or the churches;[2] it comes from Jesus Christ himself in the Holy Spirit. 'Unity' is given in him and exists in relationship to him. Jesus Christ himself cannot be divided: he is the head of his body, the church. He is the undestroyed and indestructible basis of church unity. This church unity given and existing in Christ therefore underlies all the Christian churches. However, in their divisions the churches refuse even to express this given and existing unity in visible church fellowship and worship.

Nevertheless, fundamental common convictions of the churches which do not live together in fellowship point to this given and existing church unity, and already express it in the separated churches. These convictions include the acknowledgment of the Holy Scripture of the Old and New Testament and the recognition of its priority over all church statements as an expression of persistence, or the desire to persist, in the apostolic faith; and they include the use of the creeds of the early church in the worship of the separated churches as an expression of the agreement of present-day Christianity in the universal faith of Christians down the centuries. Despite the dissolution of church fellowship, what Ephesians expresses as 'one Lord, one faith, one baptism; one God and Father of all, who is over all and through all and in all' (Eph.4.5f.) does exist.[3] This and yet other perspectives, for example the acknowledgment of its own guilt for schism,[4] were key reasons why the Second Vatican Council felt able to join in the ecumenical movement on the basis of given and existing church fellowship, which has not been destroyed even by the schisms, but up to that point had not been acknowledged by the Roman Catholic church. These perspectives are explicitly emphasized in the Dogmatic Constitution on the Church, *Lumen Gentium* (no. 15), and in the Decree on Ecumenism, *Unitatis redintegratio* (nos. 14–24). At the council they led to a positive assessment of the character of the other Christian churches as churches.

Nevertheless, these perspectives which it had regained did not allow the council wholly to leave behind the traditional ecclesiological constraints of the Roman Catholic Church of the second millennium. Even according to the texts of the Second Vatican Council, only the Roman Catholic Church is 'fully a church', whereas all the other churches – measured by the institutions, teachings and practices of the Roman Catholic Church – have only a degree of the character of the church, and in each case a lesser degree.[5] The criterion for the verdict is the Roman Catholic Church itself, and not the foundation of church fellowship as described above, to which all bear witness and by which the character of the Roman Catholic Church as church is also constituted. A quantitative, almost materialistic, understanding of the nature of being the church distorts the perception that the understanding of the church must necessarily be qualitative. The church of Jesus lives and fulfils itself in and through the churches; it is given where the word of God (Holy Scripture) is handed on in a living way in Jesus Christ as the sole word of salvation, and the 'reception of salvation by faith alone' is preached as unconditional, i.e. where the receiving of salvation is not linked to any church conditions of whatever kind.[6] This makes the church the church; everything else that there is in the churches must not distort a perception of this centre. It belongs on the side of the *bene esse* of the church, which can be evaluated differently from different perspectives. That is true even if the Roman church declares that the basic structures of its church constitution belong to the *esse* of the church of Jesus Christ. For constitutions can never claim this status for themselves, since all down Christian history from its first beginnings, the church has had different constitutions and therefore can still have today. So the Roman Catholic idea that all the other churches have 'degrees of being the church' in a quantitative sense can never legitimately be derived from the objectively given *bene esse* of the church, which is regarded subjectively in the Roman Catholic Church as belonging to the *esse* of the church. The idea of 'degrees of being the church', i.e. in fact the idea of being half, three-quarters, or 'fully' the church, is nonsensical. The idea of fullness means 'being filled with the Holy Spirit'; it has nothing to do with a positivistic and materialistic concept of fullness. Such 'being filled with the Spirit' can be served with very different church constitutions.

The Second Vatican Council rediscovered the *koinonia/communio* ecclesiology of the early church. The notion of the unity of the church as a fellowship of independent churches can be rethought with the help of this ecclesiology. However, the ecclesiology of the Roman centralism of the second Christian millennium has lagged behind this ecclesiology, which is to be found in the texts of *Lumen Gentium* (Chapter 3). Through Roman centralistic ecclesiology the unity of the church can be thought of only as the subordination of all the other churches to the Roman papacy. It is easy to see that the two ecclesiologies cannot be harmonized. Since Roman centralistic ecclesiology is mainly responsible for the split between the church of the East and the church of the West and the split within the Western church in the sixteenth century, it leads into an ecumenical dead end from which the Second Vatican Council consciously and deliberately wanted to extract itself. It did so by taking up the *koinonia/communio* ecclesiology of the early church. Only by referring this ecclesiology to the present situation in the church can promising ecumenical steps be taken. However, recourse to the *koinonia/communio* ecclesiology does not make sense if the intention is merely the restitution of the conditions of the early church as the conditions of the early church. But when applied to the present this ecclesiology has so many hitherto unexhausted possibilities that the outlines of an answer to the question 'Towards what unity of the churches' can be given.

II. Towards what unity of the churches?

This question has been reflected on since the beginnings of the modern ecumenical movement in the nineteenth century, and particularly during the heyday of this movement in the twentieth century.[7] The most different models of possible church unity have been developed and discussed. Most of the models developed were very closely connected with the particular understanding of the church held by those churches which accepted such concrete aims in their ecumenical work. Closely connected with this is the conceptuality chosen on each particular occasion for what was and is desired to be achieved. It is first worth noting this conceptuality.

One term for the goal of ecumenical work used in the earlier ecumenical literature, and not just in the Roman Catholic literature, is a 'reunion of the Christian churches'. This term has long – and rightly – disappeared from ecumenical literature. The term 'reunion' implies an understanding of the church and church life as it is lived in practice which does not accord with historical reality. It presupposes that there was a church which possibly had a strict organization, which was universal and led by Rome, from which the confessions had separated and which now had to be united with Rome. It was Patriarch Athenagoras who, if I am right, finally dismissed this term in 1964. When asked by a reporter from the French Roman Catholic journal *La Croix*, 'Do you believe that there will soon be reunion with the Roman Church?', Athenagoras replied: 'We were never united.' He then went on to tell the astonished questioner: 'We lived together in fellowship and we will continue to live in fellowship.'[8]

No less problematical than the term reunion is the term unity itself, whether in the phrase 'unity of Christians', in the phrase 'unity of the church', or even in the phrase 'unity of the churches'.[9] The concept of unity can never lose the totalitarian features which are intrinsic to it and which have existed in history; moreover, it is a purely static term which does not adequately reflect the dynamic and life of the churches. The term unity points far more to a realm of the dead than to a living church. But if it has to be used in connection with ecumenical aims, it must never be used by itself, but only in connection with multiplicity: 'unity in multiplicity', 'unity through multiplicity', 'multiplicity in unity'. However, as these phrases are very formal and, to judge from the ecumenical dialogues so far, have succeeded in indicating only an emphasis on unity in a multiplicity which is vague, diffuse, unappreciated and articulated only verbally, rather than emphasizing the multiplicity in unity, they are not much use in answering the question which forms the title of this article. Combined with the term multiplicity, however, the term unity may indicate what is designated by the term *koinonia, communio*, fellowship.[10] This term can express more appropriately than any other terms what 'unity of the churches' is to be realized, with respect both to the history of the churches and to the goal that is striven for.

In view of what happened in the first millennium of the Christian church, the term *koinonia/communio/*fellowship of the churches can put this period in too romantic a light, but it does express the idea of the independence of churches and the intrinsic bond between them. Even if for reasons which will not be discussed here the pre-Chalcedonian churches of the ancient East are later to be found only in the context of the history of the four patriarchates of the Eastern church and the one patriarchate of the Western church, and are no longer in *koinonia* with the latter, the history of the Pentarchy, full of tension and conflict, shows that the independence or autocephaly of the church and the bond of these independent churches under the idea of *koinonia* can be held together. This is also attested by the concept of catholicity in the creeds of the early church, which see the catholicity of the church given by the fact that the churches stand together 'in communion'. In these churches standing together in communion, the 'catholic faith' is attested, i.e. a faith which is shared by all, regardless of the fact that there are ways of believing in it which are not shared by all and do not even need to be shared by all.[11]

The faith which is shared by all includes worship in the whole plurality of its liturgies and forms; diakonia and the practice of hospitality; the canon of Holy Scripture in its multiplicity, which is not free from tension and contradiction, as the declared will of the churches to remain faithful to the apostolic testimony; and the creeds and ministries associated with the apostolic witness (these were pluriform in the primitive and early church; later more harmonious, but no less differentiated, albeit in another way which was always adapted to the social environment). If the early-church *koinonia* between the churches expressed here is transferred to the church today, also preserving these criteria as modes of behaviour for today, the *koinonia* of the churches which now exist would be possible, because they agree on these criteria and modes of behaviour: they remained independent yet lived in fellowship. However, on the premises of a papalist centralist Roman ecclesiology of the Western church of the second century it is impossible to think of independence and communion together, because this ecclesiology can only think of one single church, the visible principle of unity in which is the papacy with its claims to universal jurisdiction. Other ecclesiological concepts of the Western church before the Reformation, and even the Roman Catholic Church after the Reformation, have been increasingly repressed in favour of centralism.

In the Western church the idea of independent churches – with reference to the churches of the first millennium – has in fact been developed only in the Protestant churches, the Anglican Church and the Old Catholic Church. These attest that the idea of independence was attractive not only in the East but also in the West. The ecumenical movement, into which the churches have entered, is now seeking to restore the *koinonia* of these churches. It exists between the Lutheran and Reformed Churches in the Leuenberg Agreement of 1973 and between the Anglican and Old Catholic Churches in the Bonn Agreements of 1931; basic agreements have been arrived at between the Old Catholic Church and the churches of the Evangelical Church in Germany (the 1988 Meissen statement); similar agreements are also being prepared between the Anglican Church and the Lutheran Church of Sweden and the Lutheran Churches in Germany (Porvoo, Dresden). Church communion exists between the Evangelical Church of the Union and the United Church of Christ in the USA (1980/1981).[12] Moreover in 1987 the Protestant Church in Germany agreed on full communion, including preaching and the sacraments, with the Evangelical Methodist Church.[13] The many church networks in the USA and Canada, in India, and in South Africa, along with the national Christian councils founded all over the world and the continental church ecumenical institutions, are impressive testimony to the growing sense among Christians and in the churches of the need to restore a *koinonia* from which no one any longer wants to dissociate themselves. This feeling in itself has changed the churches decisively by comparison with their former condition, even when lamentable counter-movements in the churches often continue to clamour loudly for 'believing against one another' instead of 'believing with one another'. The future cannot belong to these voices, because this attitude is deeply contradictory to the attitude of faith itself. Because it is deeply contrary to faith not to live in *koinonia*, the question must be asked whether the *koinonia* of the churches must not urgently be opened up with reference to the criteria and modes of conduct in the early church as described above. Must not in fact more be called for than what made it possible for the churches to live in fellowship at that time? Where is worship not celebrated in the churches? Where are the creeds not said? Where is there dispute as to the status of Holy Scripture? Where is the Word of God not publicly preached and handed down in a living way, despite all human frailty? The only thing which is really undeveloped, and in some churches has not been developed at all, is hospitality and help between churches. This had pride of place in the early church. Have people ever noted that in the Roman Catholic Church a collection was held for communities of other churches which were in distress? The biblical collection for the community in Jerusalem must be rediscovered for the Christianity of the churches as it is really lived out.

The concept and substance of *koinonia* between the churches is based in communion with God through Jesus Christ in the Holy Spirit. Because they have communion with Jesus Christ, in his word and in the sacraments of baptism and eucharist, they have communion with one another. Church communion is no 'more', nor can it be more, than communion with Jesus Christ. But communion with Jesus Christ is not denied by anyone to anyone else. And where Jesus Christ grants communion with himself, churches cannot refuse communion with one another. From this fundamental perspective it is also clear that the churches must have fellowship with one another. This communion consists fundamentally in the worship of the community and grows out of it. Worship of the community, in the word of God and the celebration of the sacraments which is made a real experience, does not allow the churches to remain as they in fact are at the moment. The fellowship of worship will have an effect on all the rest of the life in the churches and between the churches, at all levels: locally, regionally, on individual continents and on a global scale. It arises out of the common testimony of the faith of Christians in the world and governs the whole of *diakonia*. It is the basis for discussion and, if necessary, for decisions following that discussion, on matters which are essential for Christians today. Such fellowship develops an awareness that the communion of the church and the churches is grounded in God and not in a consensus of teaching. Furthermore, it arouses the awareness that the fact that doctrines are disputed between opposing churches does not do away with what all that is shared; it brings these doctrines into the context of the fellowship in which only that will persist which in fact can serve living faith today. Such a view calls for the development of synodal or conciliar structures within the churches and between the churches, locally, regionally and so on. Here everything that emerges from the fellowship of worship experienced in the truth can be discussed and possibly also decided on; this will be what is of burning concern for Christians, whether problems of being the church which have come down to them, or present-day problems of bearing witness to the Christian faith.

The idea of a universal council of all Christians as the office of universal church fellowship is also to be set against the background of such considerations. In view of the importance that councils have always had in the history of the churches, in the future, too, there is need for such an office of universal church fellowship, not least also so that the local churches and partial churches do not sink into regional provincialism and forget that what is needed is not only the fully committed fellowship of all Christians in one place, but also the fellowship of all Christians in all places. Whether alongside this office of universal church fellowship in the form of a council there is need of yet another office of universal church communion which is held by a small permanent representative body or which has some other form should be discussed and decided harmoniously at a council of all Christians.

The question 'Towards what unity of the churches?' which is discussed here leads us to bid farewell to a model of organic union which has long been favoured. This model can only think of the church as a single organization and has today disappeared from the ecumenical debate. In the sense developed here the model of reciprocal recognition could more aptly express the ecclesiological consequences of such recognition, with its liturgical and ecclesiological foundation. The co-operative federal model, which has long been favoured, is too lacking in the theological foundation for the common action which is called for. But the model of *koinonia/communion*/fellowship of the churches goes very well with the model of 'unity in reconciled difference', 'the one church as a conciliar community' and the view of the other Christian churches as 'sister churches'. Each of these models emphasizes important aspects. But all these models can be forgotten if Christians do not succeed in understanding the churches in which they have received the faith simply as the places in which they have heard the message of God's irrevocable and unconditional Yes to men and women in Jesus Christ, a word of God to all people, on which they can rely in life and death. It is not the churches that are the goal and content of faith, but the living God. The churches have to withdraw before him, especially where the immediacy of the relationship between God and the individual is involved. They cannot and must not interfere in this, as they keep doing, both openly and subtly. Churches which understand themselves in the way described above live in fellowship, and yet remain independent churches, each with its independent profile, as an expression of the multiplicity and life of the Spirit of God.

Translated by John Bowden

Notes

1. Weimarer Ausgabe 40/2, 521, lines 24–39; cf. ibid., lines 2–13.
2. See Paul Gerhardt, 'Befiehl du deine wege', *Evangelisches Gesangbuch* no. 361, verse 3.
3. Cf. Heinrich Fries, *Ein Glaube, eine Taufe – getrennt beim Abendmahl?*, Graz, Vienna and Cologne 1971.
4. *Unitatis redintegratio*, no. 7.
5. See a thorough analysis and criticism in Edmund Schlink, *Nach dem Konzil*, Munich and Hamburg ²1966, especially 70–124.

6. See Karl Lehmann and Wolfhart Pannenberg (eds.), *Condemnations of the Reformation Era. Do They Still Divide?*, Minneapolis 1989.

7. For details see Harding Meyer, *Ökumenische Zielvorstellungen*, Göttingen 1996. Also Peter Neuner, 'Vor dem Ende der Konsensusökumene?', in Johannes Brosseder (ed.), *Von der Verwerfung zur Versöhnung*, Hamburg and Neukirchen-Vluyn 1996, 51–79.

8. See Wilm Sanders (ed.), *Bischofsamt – Amt der Einheit*, Munich 1983, 133.

9. For a detailed account of the problem see Johannes Brosseder, Laurentius Klein and Konrad Raiser, 'Theologie der Ökumene – Ökumenische Theoriebildung', *Ökumenische Rundschau* 37, 1988, 205–21.

10. *Communion/Koinonia. Ein neutestamentlich-frühchristlicher Begriff und seine heutige Wiederaufnahme und Bedeutung. Eine Stellungnahme des Instituts für Ökumenische Forschung*, Strasbourg 1990. Similarly the article in n. 9.

11. Johannes Brosseder, *Ökumenische Katholizität* 41, 1992, 24–39.

12. Frederick Herzog and Reinhard Groscurth (eds.), *Kirchengemeinschaft im Schmelztiegel – Anfang einer neuen Ökumene?* Neukirchen-Vluyn 1989.

13. See Johannes Brosseder and Hans-Georg Lunk (ed.), *Gemeinschaft der Kirchen – Traum der Wirklichkeit?*, Zurich and Neukirchen-Vluyn 1993.

The Passion for Unity

Joseph Moingt

What sort of unity are we talking about when we talk about the unity of the church, and where do we think it could come from? From what hidden inner source or from what still distant horizon? Before looking for an answer, perhaps we should examine the motive behind the question. What passion moves us when we raise it? Is it the fact of suffering from a lack of which we are guilty, a sin of which we bear the wound and for which we recognize that we are responsible? Or is it a feeling of superiority mixed with a claim, some secret desire for power over those whom we put, for whatever reason, outside the unity of the church? Whatever the motivation might be, it would also seem to disguise a pre-understanding, a reference to a presupposed model of unity the absence and the desire for which we feel. It might be a lost benefit, thought to exist in the past in some form, which we have to recover, preferably in identical fashion; or it might be a perfection to be sought and acquired, and doubtless in some way to be invented. But in what direction? Any objective approach to the question of unity calls for a prior elucidation of the subjective problems in which we involve ourselves.

I shall begin from the idea that we would not be seeking the unity of the church were it not given us in advance. However, it has been given as a task to fulfil; it is a *passion* which has hold of us. This passion takes many forms: a suffering to be borne with patience; a demand to be satisfied and which judges us; a dynamism which supports us and takes us forward; a grace which is a gift, but not a possession. Here we shall test this idea, this prejudice, by examining first its apostolic origin, and then the distant past of the church. Rapid though this examination it may be, it should purify the motives for our research, the passion which moves it, and at the same time illuminate the present and the future of the task which falls to us, the objectives of unity to be pursued and the means to be used in the process.

Although the question relates formally to ecumenism, I shall examine it from the more modest but more fundamental perspective of systematic and dogmatic theology. I consider the unity of the church as it is affirmed in the creed, together with its holiness, to be a reality of grace which is already there, without which the church would not be the church of Christ. The church, too, is 'one', but a reality the achievement of which is always awaited from the action of the Holy Spirit. And this makes it an object of perpetual hope. I shall therefore be adopting the perspective of the 'marks' or gifts of the church. These are gifts which are not title deeds of ownership; they are characteristics which are necessary, yet constantly need to be acquired. This resolutely eschatological perspective should warn us against the temptation of legalism, which threatens the consideration of and the quest for unity.

The proof that the unity of the church is both a gift received and a gift to be received, an actual state and a good to be achieved, is the last prayer of Christ to his Father: 'That they may all be one as you and I are one'. This is a prayer which was heard as soon as it was made, but was no less entrusted to the good pleasure of the Father. It is a prayer which is a testament in every sense of the word: the last dispositions and last will of the dying man for the benefit of his heir, but also as a charge on them. By these they enter into his heritage and receive the pledge of his gift to come. The numerous exhortations to unity which St Paul addresses to his communities give the same teaching: it is the major virtue that Christians must practise to become 'one body'. From now on it is the original and intrinsic character of the church as 'body of Christ'. That shows that unity is an immanent necessity for the church, its present status, and the law of its future, but without prejudice to its content or its form.

From the beginning the content of this unity is given essential features, but there are not many of them. From the Gospels and the letters of Paul we can sum them up in two words, in a specifically Pauline formula: the unity of the church is 'the bond of faith and love' which brings together its members 'in one spirit and one body'. Those whom Jesus calls to live in unity are those whom he himself has chosen and whom the Father has entrusted to him, those who have kept his word and to whom he has revealed the Father, and thus those who have believed in him and have learned a new way of beliving in God from him. And this precept of unity is expressed in equivalent terms in Jesus' 'new commandment' to love one another: to take care of one another, as Paul will put it, as members of the same body. We can make more specific this content of faith which is expressed in the repetitive and almost codified formulation transmitted in teaching or in liturgy, for example all the titles by which Christ is called. These beyond question already have a normative value, since we find them in the different communities at this time. It is also possible to specify the content of the love which makes up the unity of the church and to say, for example, that it implies the recognition of apostolic authority, obedience to the pastors in charge of the community, regular attendance at assemblies, a concern for the common good which takes the form of each individual exercising his or her charismas and respecting those of others, and a certain organization of ministries to the same end. All these indications are valuable, since they aim at the essential thing which makes the church one. However, they do not prescribe what institutional form, what type of statutory organization, this unity must take.

It should in fact be clear, as clear as the New Testament call to unity in faith and love, that we do not find any sketch of an authoritative and regulated unification of the different elements which make up the reality of the church, doctrine, liturgy, discipline or hierarchy. Outside his teaching of the kingdom ('in parables') and the mission of witness entrusted to his apostles, Jesus does not bind the latter by a 'testament' to any dogmatic corpus, legislative code, ritual or blueprint of power. Certainly the apostles will have been concerned to organize their communities under all these aspects, but first, for a long time this organization was to remain embryonic (we know almost nothing, for example, about their sacramental practices); and on the other hand, above all we find no institutionalized articulation of these communities, whereas we put that first in speaking today of the unity of the church. For St Paul, 'the church of Christ' is there in its oneness and its totality in every church brought together by the bond of faith and love and united to the others by the same bond, without his feeling the need to give an organized 'form' to this oneness and totality, except for the 'care' which leads him ceaselessly to travel from one community to another.

That is not to say that the different elements in the organization of the current life of the churches could not base their legitimacy on some teachings or practices of the Gospels or apostles – far from it. My argument is limited to the observation that there is no pre-established 'model' of unity.

The later tradition of the church would set itself to supplying this lack – if we must use this word to denote an absence of unifying form. In fact the absence would be experienced as a lack when a need was felt for a more extended and more authoritarian unification, to confront the disagreements over faith and the antagonisms between Christian communities. Then there is a concern to see the churches brought together as one, and to achieve that, unitary institutions are set up: creeds, 'ecumenical' councils, dogmatic definitions, canonical legislation, a hierarchical organization . . . But that only happened slowly and progressively.

To begin with and for several centuries, the Christians showed no desire to give an organic and visible, instrumental form to their unity of faith and love. They did not experience this unity any less intensively, but in the form of dissemination – the etymological sense of the word 'catholic'. Christians who were dispersed all over the place knew that they came from the same apostolic stock (I would not say the same cutting, as Tertullian said), fruits of the same seed of the gospel; and they awaited the perfect crowning of their unity from the kingdom of God. The faith in the 'one and holy' church which the third article of the so-called Apostles' Creed makes us profess, the globally eschatological focus of which cannot be challenged in the first centuries, does not relate to the earthly church. It is directed towards the church above, the heavenly Jerusalem (probably thought of at the time as a pre-existent aeon), to which the Christians 'of the last times' knew themselves 'called' by eternal election, to enter 'on the last day'. The transfer to the earthly church of the endowments of the heavenly church (this took place in the fourth century and doubtless before, under the pressure of schisms, particularly Donatism) can be, but is not necessarily, the mark of a more enlightened faith in the implications of the incarnation, the visible manifestation of the unity of the church, as of its holiness. It is to be awaited rather than constructed, and the obstinate will to arrive there sooner and to a greater degree can conceal a lack of eschatological hope as a result of an idolatry of the visible.

The concern to give the churches, hitherto independent (to different degrees) and jealous of their autonomy (often considered as a sign of apostolicity), a visible form of gathered unity, of ecumene, begins to manifest itself more clearly in the fourth century. It was in this century that the first two councils which are specifically called 'ecumenical' met. This enterprise of unification, which was to last for several centuries, calls for moderated judgments.

It was at this time that Christianity saw opening up before it the hitherto undreamed-of destiny of becoming the religion of the empire. Suddenly it moved radically from its original eschatological expectation and sought to implant itself more durably and solidly in time, like earthly empires and with their support. This was, fatally, to lead to a reciprocity in services rendered. Uniformity in professions of faith and religious practices, obedience imposed on decisions with universal scope, taken in distant centres, sometimes at the cost of the abandonment of immemorial local traditions, the organization of local churches into administrative groupings, centralized and hierarchical, were all measures which contributed to the unity of a church which now conceived of itself as having imperialist dimensions and universalistic pretensions. But they were equally useful to an empire which often imposed them or supported them, albeit not without making onerous demands in return. They were measures which were perhaps useful to the propagation of Christianity (which had not expected the help of the empire in spreading in so-called 'barbarian' countries), but finally more apt for the visibility and political status of the church than for the radiation of the Gospel within believing communities, if not in the world.

So there was progress, but it was ambiguous, especially if one considers the other side of the coin; it was often these authoritative measures which aroused oppositions between parties, rivalries between episcopal sees and divisions between churches, and which engendered schisms, many of which have lasted to the present day. Unity was achieved, but at the cost of exclusions and amputations, at the cost of a 'fragmentation' of the totality. In the end a certain regional 'catholicity' was constructed at the expense of ecumenicity. In bitter fights over 'orthodoxy', the purity and understanding of the faith doubtless came out on top, at least to a certain point, but love bore wounds from them which have not been effaced. There can be no authentic progress in unity where love does not grow alongside faith.

This survey of earliest times, when the whole, but unlimited, content of the unity of the church was a seed of faith nourished by love; and of the past, when it began to give itself the form of an authoritarian totality, but one which broke up to the degree that it sought to reinforce and extend itself, should have taught us that the passion for unity must not be some political will like that by which nations or states are constructed. Jesus sometimes warned his disciples against this temptation, and the church's difficulties in the course of its history should dissuade it from the dreams to which it could succumb, for whatever good motives.

The unity of the church, conceived of as the gathering together of all Christians in a centralized institution under a single command, is not required as such by any law of the gospel and has existed only in a state of fragmentation. In some historical configurations of society, this political model has been able to present itself as a means of arriving at the ideal form of unity. Its repeated failures make us more sceptical today, when we have a better grasp of the resistance of cultures to the many forms of imperialism. It has been thought that this model best realized the will of Christ to gather all his sheep into one fold under the watch of one shepherd. But that is only one interpretation among other possible ones of an allegory which one would hesitate to put forward as an ideal form of obedience for modern Christians. In his time St Cyprian was able to present the monarchical form of the churches of his time as the sacrament of the unity of the Trinity. That applied only to the local churches and excluded their subordination to some external authority. Bringing together the greatest possible number of Christians under the purest form of monarchianism, the Roman church has long conceived of itself as the one church of Christ which one day all Christians throughout the world must join. At Vatican II it again asked itself questions about this point, marked by the ideology of the *societas perfecta*; it emerged from its isolation, recognized the at least potential ecclesiality of the other Christian confessions, and regarded itself as a 'pilgrim' people in the midst of the others, 'a church always in need of being reformed'. That was not a renunciation of unity but an invitation to take new ways.

For Christ's precept never ceases to instil in us the passion for unity, which cannot be content with shams or cheap measures. The important thing is to see by what means we can go most surely and furthest along this way. To think the unitary form of authority necessary to the oneness of the disclosure of faith is again to yield to the prestige of the monarchical ideal and to confuse the unity of faith with that of discourse. For faith, as for anything else, it is culture which brings about the unity of discourse, regarded as conceptual systematization. A critical re-reading of the history of dogma shows that the unity of the faith is most frequently broken at this level of dogmatic representations, not understood by the mass of faithful, even when their faith remained intact. If one had to judge by this standard, how many Catholics today would be counted in the unity of the church? But the faith of those who were once called 'the simple' and are now called 'the poor', used to be spoken of in other terms. Is it right to apply a more rigorous standard to the faith of other Christians, thought to be outside this unity because they use a different language?

Before being assent to a dogmatic corpus, faith is a matter of going through the Gospel listening to Christ, the event of an encounter with him, trust in him as saviour, an awareness of the singular bond which unites him to God. It is the experience of the Holy Spirit in sharing in the existence of other Christians, participation in their sacramental life, slow dialogue with them, which brings growth in understanding of the faith, and a common practice of the gospel precepts. It is at this level that the unity of faith must primarily be found, a level which has its roots in love. It does not impose itself primarily in the form of a discourse imposed from outside or above; it comes about in a communion of life, faith and love. At the grass roots, the *sensus fidei* takes shape in communication between believers. To want to establish or extend unity between all the Christian confessions is to establish or extend the dialogue among Christians at every level, and primarily in the form of that basic love which is the recognition of their identity as Christians in the diversity of their forms of discourse. Far from being remote from this task, theological discourse puts itself at the service of this communication between believers, the presentation of the faith, before making itself the spokesman of a magisterium.

At all events, the task of constructing the unity of the church cannot be kept within its frontiers, even 'ecumenical' frontiers. Experience shows that there has been too much talk of unity, sometimes at the expense of bringing it about. Something needs to be done together which should not be just an inter-church service. Common action is needed to bring about the unity of humankind. As Vatican II well understood, Christ calls all men and women, all people on earth, to enter his one church, and that is why it will never be able to find a perfect or definitive form in this time of the world. To proclaim Christ as universal brother and God as common father of all men and women, the church cannot keep to a discourse of faith; it must give a visible testimony of love and put itself at the service of the world, as Vatican II also said. To work for the peace and liberation of the peoples, for the promotion of the dignity of persons, their rights and freedoms, for equality in sharing the resources of the earth among all people, is the task for and in which Christians should gather together. By working for the unity of the world, Christian will achieve union among themselves, and the unity of the church will come about in the brotherly communion of peoples as individuals: a passion for the unity of the church, the task of humanizing the world.

Translated by John Bowden

The Unity of the Church through the Unity of Humankind

Giuseppe Ruggieri

The beginnings of a new understanding

Bonhoeffer, in his famous 'Thoughts on the Day of the Baptism of Dietrich Wilhelm Rüdiger Bethge',[1] said that he was convinced that Christians had to begin once again, as at the beginning of their history, to understand the meaning of the great words of their tradition, since these had become difficult and remote for the men and women of his time. And he looked forward to the dawning of a day when people could once again speak the word of God in such a way that the world would be changed and renewed.

When Bonhoeffer formulated these thoughts, he was moved above all by the incapacity of the church and Christians generally to speak words which had meaning and could arouse people in the face of the great parade of evil and Nazi inhumanity. Today the situation has changed. Like him, we are experiencing the need for a new 'beginning of understanding', but for very different reasons. The barbarism of our time is not that of the Nazis. But humanity is equally caught up in manifestations of violence; these have various origins: ethnic, religious fundamentalist and economic. And the disintegration of the great ideologies and the certainties which dreamed of the reconciliation of humankind under a single ideal of brotherhood and equality has resulted in an unprecedented range of diversity. So the great words of the Christian tradition have to be understood again in depth if they are to be effective. Even the confession of 'one church' which Christians proclaim in their creed runs the risk of no longer having a comprehensible content.

The culture of otherness

The attempt to identify what are called epoch-making or structural changes or the like is certainly a risky one. The significance of these changes in fact often emerges only over a period of time, and quite often what seemed to be changes of a long duration prove to be only passing phases. Indeed historians dealing with long periods advise us not to see earth-shaking events everywhere. So it is only with great caution that one can make some statements about the present time and the future which confronts us. However, despite this necessary circumspection, it does seem that various signs are indicating with sufficient certainty in our time the establishment of two quite contradictory phenomena.

On the one hand the earth is becoming an increasingly global village, with an increasingly unified language, and with the possibility of ever-increasing communication 'in real time', for which distances are totally abolished and every man and every woman can from their own room become 'contemporary' with any person or event taking place anywhere on the face of the planet.

However, on the other hand, despite this globalization of human relationships, or perhaps thanks to them, a different pattern of otherness is emerging. In the very period in which ethnic differences and religious fundamentalisms seem to be establishing themselves as causes of violence, a new 'innocence' seems to be springing up in the world, a desire for profound peace with creation, an ultimate legitimation of the 'different' and the 'other'. The ideal of a certain kind of Enlightenment modernity, that of a subject capable of dominating, transforming and assimilating everything solely by the capacity of critical reason, in a position to grasp all the particularities of human experience, is in fragments. This experience presents itself in irremediably fragmentary form and it is impossible to reconstitute it in a single figure. The context in which life is lived keeps multiplying, and a 'fusion of horizons' does not seem possible. All we can do is to note the diversity of the worlds in which we live and the dignity in every fragment. Today a conception of human history in which the other can be recognized by virtue of being 'equal' to us seems alien, even inhuman. We have only a confused understanding of everything, even if we have not yet succeeded in giving this need an effective concrete form, in translating it into customs and institutions, and in resolving the con-tradictions which it introduces within the globalization of relationships which are not totality and identity – the key words of the world which is announcing itself to us. The innocence of humankind, not as an infantile condition, but as an achievement made at great cost, can only be that of the splendour of every human face, of the dignity of every fragment. What is needed is therefore a culture of otherness, even if in our time it is possible to speak only of a 'threatened otherness' of all the contrary signs which with no less force characterize our era.[2] For this reason, an ideal of unity which entailed, under whatever name (say that of error and sin), the inevitable exclusion of any of these fragments could only be a concession to the incapacity of human beings and the narrow-mindedness of their spirits. It would be in contradiction to 'the eternity we have received in our hearts' (Koheleth 3.11).

Christianity itself is discovering that it has to live with the other religions and face them, recognizing them not, as was customary in the past, as 'works of the devil', but as places in which the Spirit is at work. Furthermore, contemporary Christianity is discovering that its own experiences of faith cannot be reduced to other experiences which follow other rhythms and draw on other spirits, maintaining their positivity and plausibility. And above all, Christians are discovering the 'non-place' of the language of faith, in the sense that Michel de Certeau gave to this expression: even within countries which have a Christian tradition there is not a social body which can articulate itself in the language of faith.[3] That is, even within the social body itself, and still more in the planetary context, there is such a cultural polycentrism, such a plurality of points of reference in various human experiences, that the claim of a single cultural synthesis, even if limited to one's own time, is proving illusory. Rather, the contemporary horizon of Christian experiences is determined by religious pluralism, the disappearance of the 'social body' of Christian language, the plurality of cultures and contexts of life. Here is a situation in which every fragment shines with its own light. In that situation, what meaning does the unity of the church have?

The ecclesial 'sign' of unity

The question should not be thought a naive one. In fact the unity of the church, the unity that is professed in the Niceno-Constantinopolitan Creed, is in close symbiosis with the aspirations to unity present in human history. So when these aspirations to unity take on a different configuration, the conception of church unity is conditioned by them. The desire for unity among human beings and the need to exorcize the threat to this unity which derives from the potential of violence in the diversity of individuals and groups are not elements extraneous to that mystery of unity which Christians believe is at work in their church through the Spirit of Christ. And at least this is the conviction expressed by Vatican II when it asserts that 'the church is in Christ as a sacrament or a sign and an instrument of intimate unity with God and the unity of the whole human race' (*Lumen Gentium* 1). The council is convinced that the unity of the church lies at the level of the sign, of sacramentality. The sign is not an autonomous reality, but is a 'reminder' of something else. That does not mean that the sign is a simple signal which is therefore only a conventional indication. In fact the council puts the sign below the category of 'sacrament'; and this always contains a 'presence'. Sacramental celebrations always imply the experience of a mystic reality which is 'given' to those who participate in them. But that does not disguise the fact that the sacramental signs have their own centre outside themselves, that the presence of the mystery experienced in them is a function of a reality (which the ancient scholastics called *res*) which is in the sacrament only in the initial stage and then has to be realized in the actual life of human beings. The peace and the communion experienced in the eucharistic celebration are, for example, a function of the communion and the peace which are experienced in everyday life.

The truth of the sign

To class the unity experienced and confessed in the churches as a sign does not mean reducing it to a mere cipher. An awareness of the inadequacy of our past conceptions should make us ask about their very basis, about the truth of the unity which we experience in the sacrament of the church. One cannot return to the beginnings of understanding at the expense of the truth of dogma.

The unity experienced in the church as a reflection of the first Christian communities always has a theological basis. Whether it is located in the body and blood of the one eucharist (I Cor. 10.16–17; 11.27, 29) or is conceived of as the work of the one Spirit, but also of the one Father and the one Son (Eph. 4.3–6),[4] this unity is always seen as a necessary consequence of a characteristic of God which Christians recognize. Because God is in a certain way, i.e. is one, those who refer to him cannot but live in the bond of peace (Eph. 4.3). This is the peace which is Christ himself (Eph. 2.14), who with the gift of his life has reconciled human beings with God and has made them neighbours of one another.

To put oneself at the beginnings of understanding therefore means to rethink all the possibilities contained in the advent of God in Jesus Christ, so as not to limit this possibility to a figure of unity which was conditioned by the culture of totality and identity. Now in Christ the unity of God appears as the welcoming of diversity. There is in fact no greater diversity, in respect of God, than sin, and Christ died for us specifically *while* we were sinners (Rom. 5.8). The unity which God brings about with humankind is not the fruit of their conversion to him, but stands at the beginning of that conversion and makes it possible.

To begin from what appears to be the unity that the churches should realize should not be in itself the fruit of their reconciliation, but what makes it possible. Only within a culture of identity does a conception of unity as the fruit of assimilation, a conception which still seems to be dominant in so many Christians and in so much of the ecumenical movement itself, make sense. Unity with the other, as a welcome of his or her otherness, is not a concession, a failure to go as far as the demands of truth, but is a welcome of that truth which God has shown to human beings in Jesus Christ.[5] And in a lecture given in 1982, Karl Rahner made a prophecy which perhaps has yet to be heard by the church:[6] the role of the Spirit in history leads us to discover that the churches already have sufficient elements of unity (the scriptures and the Niceno-Constantinopolitan Creed), so that all that is lacking is a decision for reunification. We cannot in fact fail to feel unity 'as such a radical obligation deriving from Jesus Christ, that we have the courage to put in second place many perplexities which are not in themselves irrelevant'.[7]

Unity in the church

However, again beginning from the event of Jesus of Nazareth as it is presented in the interpretation of the New Testament, it is important to emphasize another aspect, even before unity between different churches. This is the unity experienced within each church, of which unity between the churches is the coherent and logical manifestation. If in fact Christian unity is the unity of the very mystery of God as this has been manifested through Jesus of Nazareth, then it cannot be reduced to a 'mark' of the church. The theology of the 'marks' carries with it all the legacy of controversies, and was developed in connection with establishing a particular identity over against the other confessional identities.[8] The unity of the church then transfers itself from its original context, that of the profession of faith which proclaims the mystery of the unity brought about by the Spirit, into the context of reciprocal polemic. The first major theological reflection which withdrew from this narrow horizon was that of J. B. Möhler in 1825, which significantly was entitled 'Unity *in the Church*'.[9] The unity that we in fact profess in the creed is not something that the church could have, but is a unity which the Spirit of Christ brings about in the church and is also a unity which transcends it. It will only be revealed in its fullness in the final reconciliation, when God is all in all. In Möhler, the mystery is rethought in the romantic context of the organic unity of the universe. Within a culture of otherness, where the other is affirmed, recognized and welcomed in his or her diversity, the unity which the Spirit of Christ brings about in the church is understood more as a capacity for relationship, just as Christ was capable of entering into a relationship with all human beings, even with sinners. We can even say that the Christ event was ultimately the advent of a 'global' relationship, a being for others. In Christ the unity which God posits in the history of human beings in fact takes the form of being for other men and women, without exception.

An understanding of Christian unity which did not go deeper into the christological event of relationship as the advent of God in history would be obliged to borrow its basic categories from elsewhere. In the existence of Jesus, from his humble birth to his abandonment on the cross, we find the exegesis of the depth of God and at the same time the narrative of the mystery which has been put into the heart of all human beings. To have a new understanding of unity is to have a new understanding of the meaning of Jesus the Christ in our time. But this implies a remaking of christological reflection. Moreover the theological debate on non-Christian religions shows sufficiently the lack of an effective relational christology. This is the reason why the acceptance of other religious experiences does not succeed in grasping the real relationship (albeit not inclusive) with the christological event.[10]

Starting from this event, the essence and existence of the church are justified as a function of the way of human beings towards unity, in the concrete form which this sometimes takes in history. But this is not the sense in which the church should 'gather' all human beings within itself, healing their differences. The churches are in fact also a 'fragment' of human history, but reconciled with God. The unity which the Spirit brings in the fragment of the church can therefore only be the opening up of the fragment, its capacity to stick together and to stick to other fragments.

This is not a generic openness to otherness. In the New Testament, the relationship which Christ establishes with others is determined by the fact that the other is 'that which was lost', the sinner, the poor. Jesus says of himself that he has not come to call the righteous, but sinners (Matt. 9.13ff.). So he has come to break down the last barrier that human beings raise to justify their rejection of otherness, that of ethics. The horizon of the Beatitudes is not ethical, but theological. As Jacques Dupont has shown, in their original meaning the Beatitudes do not describe the moral conditions for participating in the kingdom of God, but the sovereignty of God over history which is expressed for his preference for those who have not acted in accordance with the common measure of human valuations.[11]

The unity professed in the church is thus experienced, not when the logic of identity and the exclusion of difference is dominant in it, but when, in obedience to the Christ who died for us while we were still sinners, it preaches the mercy of God for all men and women and relates itself to those who have no place at the table of others.

Questions

The understanding of unity which I have developed, albeit only roughly, is clearly naive and even risks being utopian. It is not in fact easy and perhaps not even realistic to think that the churches will accept living in the humility of the fragment, open to the other fragment. They are too rich in their own pasts to be able to speak the words of Peter easily to the people of their time: 'I have no silver or gold, but I give you what I have; in the name of Jesus Christ of Nazareth, walk' (Acts 3.6). Their confessional identities, often acquired with the blood of martyrs, are too strong for the churches to be able to renounce 'absoluteness' (in the literal sense of the term *absolutus*, i.e. the loosening of bonds) from what they have become. The radicalism of the gospel, capable of reshaping in concrete and present experience the words of unity which God brought about on the cross, and which contrasts with the past, is tolerated within the church but does not succeed in leaving its mark on the face of the globe. Rather, it seems destined to be the exclusive privilege of some men and women, even of some groups, but does not succeed in characterizing their institutions, their doctrinal systems and their pastoral strategies. Thus the question arises whether the mystery of unity within the churches and among the churches can be experienced more in accordance with a configuration which is closer to the gospel on the one hand and truly meaningful for a culture of otherness on the other.

The past, marked by the great doctrinal struggles and the dialectic between orthodoxy and heterodoxy, will seem increasingly different. It is possible to cite some obvious signs of this change in the doctrinal situation: the Catholic church and the Assyrian (Nestorian) church have made an agreement which states that the condemnations of the past arise out of misunderstandings; the Byzantine church and the Catholic church have repealed their respective excommunications;[12] Catholics and Lutherans are discussing how to establish whether the reciprocal condemnations of the sixteenth century still have any meaning.[13] Even if these agreements do not lead to the re-establishment of communion, they, too, are a good indication of the climate of friendship and mutual respect. The changes at a doctrinal level do not so far seem to indicate a different understanding of the Christian sayings about unity. The reason for this should perhaps be sought in the fact that the churches feel called to reformulate their role in societies which are increasingly secularized, rather than to have a new understanding of the words of the gospel.

To understand the problem it is necessary to pay attention to the fact that what seems to be the deepest mark of the great churches, in their internal organization and in mutual relationships, is the quest for a new role in civil society. In fact secularized societies, at the very moment in which they are experiencing the multiplication of different worlds, are in search of a basic meaning which only the great religious institutions seem capable of giving. To quote the words of della Baviera, the Italian Minister of Culture:

> What is the significance of the faith and the church today? Despite a diagnosis which might seem rather to suggest the disappearance of illusions, in my view it is wrong to give up. In my view, as a politician aware of his responsibilities in this situation, it is meaningful and necessary to defend in our country the strong position of the two great Christian confessions, not only in the interest of the church but rather because it is also in the interest of our state. What the state guarantees the churches, from legal protection to economic assistance, is not in fact an act of beneficence towards them. If we reflect a little, it is clear that by acting in this way the state is doing itself a 'favour'. It is evident that the churches, yesterday as today, are very important factors of integration in our society and in our state. In fact they stabilize the political culture, transmitting values and a sense of values to a large number of men and women. In this way they not only give support to individuals, but also form a counterbalance to the increasingly pronounced individualization and atomization of our societies.[14]

If the churches accede to this request (and everything suggests that they are already doing so), it is evident that the unity which they offer to present-day society will become that of the recognition of common ethical values. The mystery of the unity professed in the Creed, the 'subversive' memory of the unity which God established with sinners in Christ, will not have the character of public testimony on the part of the churches, a contribution which only they can make to the construction of unity among men and women, but will remain confined within them, as the radical experience of some women and some men. It is no coincidence that whereas in the past the unity of the church was centred on the great doctrinal formulae, today it seems to be based on the common 'religious' recognition of some values of which societies particularly feel the need.

Thus the historical situation is that of 'the beginning of understanding'. The gospel of the cross, of the reconciliation of God with sinners, still calls for our creative imagination.

Translated by John Bowden

Notes

1. Dietrich Bonhoeffer, *Letters and Papers from Prison*, ed. E. Bethge, London 1971, 294–319.

2. G. Ruggieri, 'Gott – ein Fremder in der Kirche?', in P. Hünermann, *Gott – ein Fremder in unserem Haus. Die Zukunft des Glaubens in Europa*, Freiburg, Basel and Vienna 1996, 153f.

3. Cf. above all two of his articles, 'La rupture instauratrice' and 'Du corps à l'écriture, un transit chrétien', now in *La faiblesse de croire*, ed. L. Girard, Paris 1987, 183–226, 267–303.

4. M. Barth, *Ephesians 4–6*, Garden City, NY 1974, 464–7.

5. For a deeper treatment of the ideas indicated here, see two of my articles: 'Pour une logique de la particularité chrétienne', in J. Vermeylen, *Culture et théologies en Europe, Jalons pour un dialogue*, Paris 1995, 77–108; 'La verità crocifissa fra Trinità e storia. Per una determinazione del rapporto tra verità e comunione', *Cristianesima nella storia* 16, 1995, 318–403.

6. 'Was kann realistischerweise Ziel der ökumenischen Bemühungen um die Einheit im Glauben sein?' given in Bamberg in 1982 and then taken up and developed in H. Fries and K. Rahner, *Einigung der Kirchen – reale Möglichkeit*, Freiburg, Basel and Vienna 1983.

7. Ibid., 17.

8. Cf. the now classical work of G. Thils, *Les notes de l'Église dans l'Apologétique depuis la Réforme*, Gembloux 1937.

9. *Die Einheit in der Kirche oder das Prinzip des Katholizismus dargestellt im Geist der Kirchenväter der drei ersten Jahrhunderten*, Tübingen 1925.

10. It might be necessary here to develop these emphases, and above all to clarify how this relational christology is authentically theological and thus, in a Christian sense, trinitarian. It might also be necessary to clarify how this is a historical and practical hermeneutic, in other words the work of the Spirit of Christ which, in every age, introduces men and women to the truth. It might also be necessary to develop a specific logic, like that of a 'particular event', but one that is capable of being 'translated' universally because of its capacity to enter into relations with the other particular features of human history. Some developments in this direction can be found in my article 'La verità crocifissa' (n. 5).

11. J. Dupont, *Les Béatitudes*, Paris [2]1969.

12. For an up-to-date account of the dialogue between the Western churches and the Eastern churches see 'Chalkedon in der ökumenischen Diskussion', *Zeitschrift für Theologie und Kirche* 92, 1995, 207–37.

13. K. Lehmann and W. Pannenberg (eds.), *Condemnations of the Reformation Era. Do They Still Divide?*, Minneapolis 1989.

14. Quotation from the text distributed to European Catholic theologians who took part in a reception for the minister on 30 August 1995.

Contributors

MIKLÓS TOMKA was born in 1941; he studied economics and sociology in Budapest, Leuven and Leiden, and taught in Budapest, where he is now Professor of the Sociology of Religion. He has also been a visiting professor in Bamberg and Innsbruck. A co-founder of the Hungarian Pastoral Institute (in 1989), he is also Director of the Hungarian Catholic Social Academy and head of the Hungarian Religious Research Centre (both also from the same year).

Address: H–1171 Budapest, Váviz u.4, Hungary

JOHANN REIKERSTORFER was born in Ybbs, Austria in 1945. He studied philosophy and theology in St Pölten and Vienna, and afterwards in Louvain, where he gained his doctorates in 1970 and 1974. After his Habilitation in 1977 he taught in the Catholic Theological Faculty of the University of Vienna, where since 1979 he has been Professor of Fundamental Theology. His books include: *Offenbarer Ursprung. Eine Interpretation der Anthropologie Carl Werners*, Vienna 1972; *Die Zweite Reflexion. Über den Begriff der Philosophie bei Anton Günther*, Vienna 1974, and *Kritik der Offenbarung. Die 'Idee' als systemtheoretisches Grundprinzip einer Offenbarungstheologie: Anton Günther in Begegnung mit Johann Sebastian von Drey*, Vienna 1977.

Address: Universität Wien, Katholisch-Theologische Fakultät der Pro-dekan, Schottenring 21, A 1010 Vienna, Austria.

ANGELO MAFFEIS was born in 1960 and teaches dogmatic theology in the Seminary of Brescia; he also works as a consultant to the international commission for Catholic-Lutheran Dialogue. He has written *Il ministero nella Chiesa. Uno studio del dialogo cattolico–luterano (1967–1984)*, Milan 1991.

Address: Via Bollani 20, 25123 Brescia, Italy.

Hans Dieter Betz is Shailer Mathews Professor of New Testament Studies at the University of Chicago. As his numerous publications show, his work focusses on the interpretation of the letters and theology of Paul, the Gospel tradition, especially the Sermon on the Mount, and relations between primitive Christianity and its religious and cultural environment.

Address: University of Chicago Divinity School, Swift Hall, 1025 E 58th Street, Chicago 60637, USA.

Ulrich H. J. Körtner was born in 1957 and since 1992 has been Professor of Systematic Theology in the Protestant Theological Faculty of the University of Vienna. His publications include: *Papias von Hierapolis. Ein Beitrag zur Geschichte des frühen Christentums*, FRLANT 133, Göttingen 1983; *The End of the World* (1988), Louisville 1995; *Theologie in dürftiger Zeit. Ein Essay*, Munich 1990; *Der inspirierte Leser. Zentrale Aspekte biblischer Hermeneutik*, Göttingen 1994; *Stückweise. Fragmentarische Reflexionen über die Sinn des Lebens*, Vienna 1995; *Bedenken, dass wir sterben müssen. Sterben und Tod in Theologie und medizinischer Ethik*, Munich 1996.

Address: Institut für Systematische Theologie, Evangelisch-Theologische Fakultät der Universität Wien, Rooseveltplatz 10, A 1090 Vienna, Austria.

Lorenzo Perrone was born in 1946 and teaches early Christian literature and history at the University of Pisa. His research is into the history of the reception of Chalcedon, and monasticism and the church in Palestine in the Byzantine era. He is also interested in patristic exegesis, particularly the development of the genre of *quaestiones et responsiones*. He is co-ordinator of the Italian group researching into Origen and the Alexandrine tradition, and is involved in an international *Religious History of the Holy Land*. His books include *La chiesa di Palestina e le controversie cristologiche*, Brescia 1980; an edition of the Ethiopic text of the *Ascension of Isaiah*, and a collection of his own studies entitled *Il cuore indurito del Faraone. Origene e il problema del libero arbitrio*, Genoa 1992.

Address: Dipartimento di Filologia Classica, Via Gavani 1, 56100 Pisa, Italy.

Anne Brenon is a palaeographic archivist with a diploma in religious sciencies from the École des hautes Études. She is Conservateur du Patrimoine de France, in charge of the Centre d'Études cathares in Carcassone, and editorial secretary of the journal *Heresis*. Her books include: *Le vrai visage du Catharisme*, Toulouse 1988; *Les femmes cathares*, Paris 1992; and *Les cathares, vie et mort d'une Église chrétienne*, Paris 1996. She has also written numerous scholarly articles on Catharism and the mediaeval heresies.

Address: Maison des Mémoires, 563 Rue de Verdun BP 197, 11004 Carcassonne Cédex, France.

BERNARD PLONGERON is a priest, Research Director at the Centre National de la Recherche Scientifique and Professor at the Institut Catholique in Paris. He is also a permanent consultant on the humane sciences to the Research Council of Canada in Ottawa. His most recent books are *La vie quotidienne du clergé français au XVIIIe siècle* (²1988) and *L'abbé Grégoire ou l'arche de la Fraternité* (1989). He is at present finishing Volume 10 of the *Histoire du Christianisme: Les défis de la modernité (1770–1840)*, of which he is editor.

Address: 30 rue Saint-Placide, 75006 Paris, France.

RAIMON PANIKKAR has dedicated his life to his ministry (mainly among intellectuals) and an academic activity as Professor of Religious Studies (now Emeritus from the University of California). He continues a contemplative life retired in a small village of the pre-Pyrenees with occasional journeys to India and other parts of the world. Among his forty books are *La experiencia filosófica de la India*, Madrid 1996; *Invisible Harmony*, Minneapolis 1995; *Il daimôn della politica*, Bologna 1995; *The Vedic Experience*, Delhi 1994; *The Cosmotheandric Experience*, Mary-knoll 1993; *La Trinidad y la experiencia religiosa*, Barcelona 1989; *Myth, Faith and Hermeneutics*, Bangalore 1983.

Address: Can Felo, 08511 Tavertet (Catalunya), Spain.

PAULO SUESS was born in Cologne in 1938. He studied in the universities of Munich, Louvain and Münster, where he gained his doctorate in theology. He has lived in Brazil since 1966; since 1988 he has been head of postgraduate studies in mission in São Paulo and since 1996 Vice-President of the International Association for Mission Studies. His most important books are *Volkskatholizismus in Brasilien*, Mainz 1978; *A conquista espiritual da América Espanhola, 200 documentos – século XVI*, Petropolis 1992; *Evangelizar a partir dos projetos históricos dos outros*, São Paulo 1995.

Address: Caixa Postal 46–023: CEP 04046–970 São Paulo, Brazil.

LISA SOWLE CAHILL is Associate Professor of Christian Ethics at Boston College. She received her doctorate in theology from the University of Chicago Divinity School in 1976, after completing a dissertation entitled *Euthanasia: A Protestant and a Catholic Perspective*. Recent research interests include method in theological ethics, the use of scripture in ethics, medical ethics, and sexual ethics. Articles on these subjects have appeared in American journals such as *Theological Studies, Journal of Religious Ethics, Journal of Medicine and Philosophy, Chicago Studies, Religious Studies Review, Interpretation, Horizons*, and *The Linacre Quarterly*. She has also written *Between the Sexes: Toward a Christian Ethics of Sexuality*. She also serves as an Associate Editor of *Journal of Religious Ethics, Religious Studies Review*, and *Horizons*.

Address: Boston College, Dept. of Theology, Chestnut Hill, Mass. 02167–3806, USA.

PIERRE VALLIN was born in 1928. Since 1964 he has been professor of history and dogmatic theology, first at the Jesuit Faculty of Lyons, and then, from 1974, at the Centre Sèvres in Paris. He has been co-editor of the journals *Études* and *Recherches de Science Religieuse* (for which he writes the bulletin on ecclesiology). His main publications are: *Le travail et les travailleurs dans le monde chrétien* (1983); *Les chrétiens et leur histoire* (1985); *Histoire politique des chrétiens* (1988). He has written for *Le Canon des Écritures*, ed. C. Theobald (1990), and contributed articles on the Jesuits, Prophecy and Work to the *Dictionnaire de Spiritualité*.

Address: Centre Sèvres, 35bis Rue de Sèvres, 75006 Paris, France.

JEAN-PIERRE JOSSUA was born in Paris in 1930. He studied medicine, became a Dominican in 1953, studied theology at Le Saulchoir, and gained his doctorate at Strasbourg. He was professor and dean of faculties at Le Saulchoir until 1975. Subsequently he was director of the centre of theological formation and of the review *La Vie spirituelle*; until 1995 he was on the editorial board of *Concilium*. His most recent books are *La Foi en questions* (1989), *Le livre des signes* (1993), *Pour une historie religieuse de l'expérience littéraire* (3 vols, 1985–1994); and *Seul avec Dieu. L'aventure des mystiques* (1996). His *The Condition of the Witness* was published in English in 1985.

Address: 20 rue des Tanneries, 75013, Paris, France.

GREGORY BAUM was born in Berlin in 1923; since 1940 he has lived in Canada. He studied at McMaster University in Hamilton, Ontario; Ohio

State University; the University of Fribourg, Switzerland; and the new School for Social Research in New York. He is Professor Emeritus at the Religious Studies, Faculty of McGill University, Montreal. He is editor of *The Ecumenist*. His recent books are *Essays in Critical Theology* (1994), *Karl Polanyi on Ethics and Economics* (1996), and *The Church for Others: Protestant Theology in Communist East Germany* (1996).

Address: McGill University, 3520 University Street, Montreal, PQ, H3A 2A7, Canada.

DAVID TRACY was born in 1939 in Yonkers, New York. He is a priest of the diocese of Bridgeport, Connecticut, and a doctor of theology of the Gregorian University, Rome. He is The Greeley Distinguished Service Professor of Philosophical Theology at the Divinity School of Chicago University. He is the author of *The Achievement of Bernard Lonergan* (1970), *Blessed Rage for Order: New Pluralism in Theology* (1975), *The Analogical Imagination* (1980), and *Plurality and Ambiguity* (1987).

Address: University of Chicago, Divinity School Swift Hall, 1025 East 58th Street, Chicago, Ill. 60637, USA.

JOHANNES BROSSEDER was born in 1937; he was Professor of Systematic Theology in the Catholic Faculty of the University of Bonn from 1980 to 1988 and has held the same post in Cologne since 1988. Since September 1996 he has been President of the European Society for Ecumenical Research *Societas Oecumenica*. His publications include *Ökumenische Theologie*, Munich 1967; *Luthers Stellung zu den Juden im Spiegel seiner Interpreten*, Munich 1972; and *Rechfërtigung im Kirche*, Hamburg 1992. He is editor of Vols 10–18 of the *Internationale Ökumenische Bibliographie*, Munich and Mainz 1977–1992, and *Ökumene Konkret* (3 vols), Neukirchen-Vluyn 1992–3. He has written numerous articles on Luther, on ecumenical questions and on Christian-Jewish dialogue.

Address: Rauschendorfer Strasse 74, 53639 Königswinter, Germany.

JOSEPH MOINGT was born in 1915 and became a Jesuit in 1939. He was Professor of Systematic Theology successively at the Jesuit Faculty of Lyons-Fourvière and then at the Catholic Institute of Paris, and now holds that post at the Jesuit Faculty of the Sèvres Centre in Paris. He has been editor of *Recherches de Science religieuse* since 1968. His most recent book is *L'homme qui venait de Dieu*, Paris 1993.

Address: 15 rue Monsieur, 75007 Paris, France.

GIUSEPPE RUGGIERI teaches fundamental theology at the Studio Teologico S Paolo di Catania; he is a member of the editorial boards of *Cristianesimo nella storia* and *Concilium*. Recent publications include: *La compagnia della fede, Linee di teologia fondamentale*, Turin 1980; *Fede e cultura* (with I. Mancini), Turin 1979.

Address: Villaggio S Agata Zona B 26 B, 95121 Catania, Italy.

Concilium 1997/3

The editors wish to thank the great number of colleagues from the various Advisory Committees who contributed in a most helpful way to the final project:

J. J. Alemany	Madrid	Spain
N. Ančić	Split	Croatia
G. Baum	Montreal	Canada
W. Beuken	Leuven	Belgium
A. Carr	Chicago	USA
F. Castillo	Santiago	Chile
K. Derksen	Utrecht	The Netherlands
B. van Iersel	Nijmegen	The Netherlands
O. John	Ibbenbüren	Germany
N. Mette	Münster	Germany
R. Panikkar	Barcelona	Spain
R. Schreiter	Chicago	USA
J. E. Thiel	Fairfield	USA

CONCILIUM

The Theological Journal of the 1990s

Now available from Orbis Books

Founded in 1965 and published five times a year, *Concilium* is a world-wide journal of theology. Its editors and essayists encompass a veritable 'who's who' of theological scholars. Not only the greatest names in Catholic theology, but also exciting new voices from every part of the world, have written for this unique journal.

Concilium exists to promote theological discussion in the spirit of Vatican II, out of which it was born. It is a catholic journal in the widest sense: rooted firmly in the Catholic heritage, open to other Christian traditions and the world's faiths. Each issue of *Concilium* focusses on a theme of crucial importance and the widest possible concern for our time. With contributions from Asia, Africa, North and South America and Europe, *Concilium* truly reflects the multiple facets of the world church.

Now available from Orbis Books, *Concilium* will continue to focus theological debate and to challenge scholars and students alike.

Concilium Subscription Information - outside North America

Individual Annual Subscription (five issues): £25.00

Institution Annual Subscription (five issues): £35.00

Airmail subscriptions: add £10.00

Individual issues: £8.95 each

New subscribers please return this form:
for a two-year subscription, double the appropriate rate

(for individuals)   £25.00   (1/2 years)   . . . .

(for institutions)   £35.00   (1/2 years)   . . . .

Airmail postage
outside Europe +£10.00   (1/2 years)   . . . .

Total . . . .

I wish to subscribe for one/two years as an individual/institution
(delete as appropriate)

Name/Institution . . . .

Address . . . .

. . . .

. . . .

I enclose a cheque for . . . . payable to SCM Press Ltd

Please charge my Access/Visa/Mastercard no. . . . .

Signature . . . . .Expiry Date . . . .

Please return this form to:
SCM PRESS LTD   9 - 17 St Albans Place   London   N1 0NX